"Sheri Van Dijk has managed to successfully
principles of dialectical behavior therapy (I
friendly format. While highlighting the interplay of one's sense of self and their roles in relationships, the reader is given clear examples and skills to successfully manage their emotions and improve communication. Although the intended audience is adolescents, this book is a valuable resource for parents and anyone working with teenagers."

—**Leanne Garfinkel, MA**, clinical psychologist and dialectical behavior therapy (DBT)-informed therapist

"In this book, Sheri Van Dijk has produced a user-friendly and easy-to-understand workbook for teens struggling with relationships. The skills for healthy relationships are explained and examples given by following several teens experiencing problems. The exercises to practice the skills are presented in a way that is simple and straightforward. I will definitely recommend it to my clients."

—**Marilyn Becker MSW, RSW**, dialectical behavior therapy (DBT) skills therapist in private practice in Richmond Hill, ON, Canada

"Sheri Van Dijk has done it again! As the author of several books, she continues to inspire transformation by encouraging mindfulness, acceptance, and self-compassion. In this book intended to help teenagers with relationship skills, she explains dialectical behavior therapy (DBT) in a well-thought-out, easy-to-read manner with lots of examples. I wish I had known these skills when I was a teenager! As a therapist for over twelve years, I would also recommend this book as a valuable resource to therapists, parents, and others who support teenagers."

—**Rennet Wong-Gates MSW, RSW**, child and family therapist

"Relationships are complicated, and for many teens, the source of much distress. In this very clear and user-friendly workbook, Sheri Van Dijk shares the key components for the development and enhancement of teens' self-awareness, emotional self-management, and self-esteem—all of which positively impact the success of their relationships and connections to others. I found this workbook easy to read, and view it as a valuable resource for my teenage clients, as well as their parents."

—**Pat Counter, BA, DipCS, RSW**, social worker in the Disruptive Behaviours Program at Southlake Regional Health Centre

"After thirty years of clinical practice, I have finally found a book that helps teens to identify their feelings and learn practical skills for changing behaviors. Sheri Van Dijk offers examples that help readers truly relate to the concepts she teaches. This easy-to-read guide on improving interpersonal relationships is a necessity for any teen that wishes to lead a happier, healthier life. I will definitely recommend it to my clients."

—**Francine Mendelowitz, LCSW**, psychotherapist and founder of InterACT New York

the *i*nstant help
solutions series

Young people today need mental health resources more than ever. That's why New Harbinger created the **Instant Help Solutions Series** especially for teens. Written by leading leading psychologists, physicians, and professionals, these evidence-based self-help books offer practical tips and strategies for dealing with a variety of mental health issues and life challenges teens face, such as depression, anxiety, bullying, eating disorders, trauma, and self-esteem problems.

Studies have shown that young people who learn healthy coping skills early on are better able to navigate problems later in life. Engaging and easy-to-use, these books provide teens with the tools they need to thrive—at home, at school, and on into adulthood.

This series is part of the **New Harbinger Instant Help Books** imprint, founded by renowned child psychologist Lawrence Shapiro. For a complete list of books in this series, visit newharbinger.com.

relati*onship skills 101 for teens

your guide to dealing with daily drama, stress & difficult emotions using dbt

SHERI VAN DIJK, MSW

Instant Help Books
An Imprint of New Harbinger Publications, Inc.

Publisher's Note

Distributed in Canada by Raincoast Books

Copyright © 2015 by Sheri Van Dijk
     New Harbinger Publications, Inc.
     5674 Shattuck Avenue
     Oakland, CA 94609
     www.newharbinger.com

The Opposite Action chart, "What's Your Communication Style?" quiz, and "The Interpersonal Effectiveness Self-Assessment" are adapted with permission from DON'T LET YOUR EMOTIONS RUN YOUR LIFE FOR TEENS by Sheri Van Dijk. Copyright © 2011 by Sheri Van Dijk. Used by permission of New Harbinger Publications.

Cover design by Amy Shoup; Acquired by Tesilya Hanauer; Edited by Karen Schader

All Rights Reserved

Printed in the United States of America

Library of Congress Cataloging in Publication Data on file

17 16 15

10 9 8 7 6 5 4 3 2 1   First printing

As always, this book is dedicated first and foremost to my family. It's through my relationships with you that I have been able to help others strive to be healthier and more balanced in their own relationships.

This book is also for you, Michael. Thank you for making me laugh, and for just being you; I believe in you.

And thank you also to my clients. The relationships I form with each of you, although sometimes brief, are enriching and always teach me something; I appreciate that you allow me to be a part of your healing.

Contents

Introduction

For some people, connecting with others seems to come effortlessly. They have many friends, they date, they manage to have pretty good relationships with their parents, and they don't get bullied in school. I'm guessing that, if you've picked up this book, you're not one of those people; or you're looking for some tips on how to be more successful in your relationships. Well, you've come to the right place.

First, let's clarify what this book *isn't*. It's not a rule book; it's not a book that will emphasize the importance of going along with what your parents and everyone else in your life thinks just to help you get along more easily. Instead, it's a book that aims to help you think for yourself and specifically to think about what you can do to move closer to the relationships you'd like to have. Sometimes that might mean going along with your parents—but the emphasis here will be on making your own choices about what is in your best interest, and in the best interests of your relationships with your parents, your friends, your teachers, and whomever else you have in your life. Sometimes that will involve voicing an opinion that is contrary to the popular opinion, and the emphasis will be on speaking out instead of staying quiet, if that's what's going to help you move toward your long-term goals. In other words, the aim of this book is to help you think independently and then make healthy, positive choices, even if they're not the easy choices.

For most of us, some relationships—and for some of us, all of them!—don't come easily; it takes hard work to keep them healthy. And perhaps even working at them doesn't seem to get you anywhere. No matter how hard you try, you're the butt of jokes in school, or you can't please your parents, or you've never had a girlfriend, or you don't even have someone you could call a friend. This book will address all of these problems and more, and you'll learn some skills that will help you move closer to being the person you would like to be in your relationships. Even if you think you're pretty good at relationships, it's important to remember that there's always room for improvement. You can never be too good with people!

The Importance of Relationships

You may be a bit on the fence about this: *If it's so hard, do I really need connections with others? Wouldn't it be smarter to put my energy into other things instead?* The answer, and a part of you probably already knows this, is a resounding no—you need people in your life, and in order to get where you want to be in life, you need to work on improving how you interact with others.

It's quite common for us to be oblivious to how many things in our lives rely on our being able to communicate well with others. But remember that relationship skills aren't just about getting a date for Friday night or becoming one of the "popular" people in school; you need to have good interpersonal skills just to get along in life.

Improving your relationship skills will help you move closer to what you want in life. Relationship skills will help you reach your goals when you need to speak with your teacher about how to improve a grade or when you want to convince your parents to extend your curfew or lend you the car. As you move on in life, people skills will come in handy when you're applying for college or jobs, when you speak with a landlord about repairs that need to be done in your apartment, or when you go to a bank to get a loan for your first car. You'll need people skills to succeed at work, whether you work *for* a boss or you *are* the boss.

Hopefully you're getting an idea of how important it is to have good relationship skills. These skills not only move us closer to getting what we want in life but also improve our chances of having healthy personal relationships.

Let's look at the consequences of unhealthy relationships, or a lack of relationships. If either of these is the case for you, you'll probably notice that it has a domino effect on the rest of your life, with at least some of the following negative consequences:

- Low self-esteem

  Not feeling connected with others often causes people to feel poorly about themselves, like they don't deserve relationships or they're not good enough to be in relationships. Not having enough personal connections or having unhealthy connections to others often causes people to question their own worth.

- Feelings of sadness, isolation, and loneliness

  If you don't have others you can share things with, you'll tend to feel sad or down more often, and the resulting feelings of being isolated and lonely can add to your sadness and lead to depression.

- Increased stress

  Of course, life is full of stress: getting assignments done on time, getting along with your family and friends, figuring out what you want to do with the rest of your life, and so on. But when people feel alone in life, when they don't have others to talk to about things and feel that they have no one supporting them, life becomes even more difficult and stressful. Having people in your life whom you know you can count on to support you—even if they can't help you fix a problem—makes things more bearable.

- Lack of fulfillment

  Again, not having people to share things with in your life—the good and the bad—leads to a lack of fulfillment, a feeling of loneliness, or a feeling that something is missing in your life, which over time can lead to a depressed mood.

- Lack of self-confidence

  Not having others in your life to support and encourage you, and the low self-esteem that often results from a lack of healthy connections with others, usually also lead to a lack of self-confidence, or a lack of belief in your ability to succeed at things. This, in turn, will reduce your willingness to take risks and face challenges, as you don't believe in yourself enough to do so.

Overall, having healthy relationships results in your feeling supported by others and increases your belief in the fact that you're not alone in dealing with the problems life will throw at you. Whether it's the rumor mill at school, the stress of exam time, or dealing with the problems that arise with your parents or your friends and girlfriend or boyfriend, you'll know you have others you can turn to. And this can often make all the difference in your ability to cope with life.

Assessing Your Interpersonal Effectiveness

Some of you may still be on the fence at this point, so I think it's a good time to have you do a self-assessment to see how this book might be helpful for you.

The Interpersonal Effectiveness Self-Assessment

Read each statement carefully, and put a check mark beside each one you think describes you. You may find that a statement applies to you *sometimes*; ask yourself if it applies to you *more often than not*, and if it does, put a check mark beside it.

Satisfaction with Relationships

_____ I feel like I don't have enough people in my life (friends, supportive family members, acquaintances, mentors, and so on).

_____ I don't have anyone I can talk with about it when I have a problem I don't know how to fix.

_____ I don't have anyone I can ask to hang out with me when I have no plans on a Saturday night.

Communication

_____ People in my life tell me that I don't communicate well.

_____ People I am close to complain that I don't open up to them.

_____ I tend to end relationships because they aren't going well without trying to fix the problems first.

Unhealthy Limits

_____ I feel like I either give or take more in my relationships, rather than having a balance of give _and_ take.

_____ I feel taken advantage of in my relationships.

_____ I tend to get into unhealthy relationships (for example, having relationships with people who use drugs or drink a lot, or who get into a lot of trouble with their parents or even the police; or having relationships with people who don't treat me well, bully me, and so on).

If you put a check mark beside more statements than not, this book will definitely be helpful for you. And if you checked more statements in one section than in others, you now have some insight into which areas you'll need to start focusing on. Later in this book you'll have an opportunity to assess some of these things—like how you communicate—in more detail. For now, let's look at what kinds of skills you'll learn in this book and how they'll be helpful for you.

Dialectical Behavior Therapy

This book is based on a therapy model called dialectical behavior therapy, or DBT. I know, "Dia—what?" This is a fancy term for a treatment developed by psychologist Marsha Linehan that teaches people skills to help them be more *effective* in life—in other words, skills that will help people change things in their lives so that they're happier and healthier, and so that their lives are closer to the way they'd like them to be. I'll be using the word "effective" a lot in this book, and it's important to remember that its meaning will be different for everyone; through reading this book and learning some of the DBT skills, you'll be able to start sorting out what will be most effective for you. In this book, we'll be focusing on the following skills in a way that will help you be more effective specifically in your relationships:

- **Core mindfulness skills** will help you live your life more often in the present moment and bring acceptance to whatever your present-moment experience is. These skills will help you reduce the emotional pain in your life and feel more at peace with yourself, which will bring a sense of balance and calmness to your relationships as well. Core mindfulness skills will also help you become aware of what might be getting in the way of your having healthy relationships, so that you can work to make changes in these areas.

- **Interpersonal effectiveness skills** will help you communicate more effectively and develop healthier, more balanced relationships.

- **Emotion regulation skills** will help you manage your emotions in healthier ways so that you don't end up taking things out on the people you care about, which can obviously be damaging to relationships. You'll learn how to act in healthier ways so that you don't push people away, and so that emotions like anxiety won't get in the way of your developing, maintaining, or even improving relationships.

- **Distress tolerance skills** will help you manage crisis situations in healthier ways so that the effect on your relationships will be minimal. When we turn to unhealthy ways of coping, like lashing out at others, using substances, skipping school, and doing other things that end up making a situation worse, we often burn out the people who want to support us. When the people you care about see that you're working hard to behave in healthier ways, they'll want to help you more.

Putting It All Together

You'll read about these skills throughout this book, and it will be very important that you put them into practice as you learn them. Don't just read this book; *use* it to help you change the way you live your life! That, of course, is not an easy thing to do. You might find that you need to read the book more than once, or develop some techniques to help the material stick— for example, making really good notes as you read, doing some highlighting or sticky noting, or putting reminders in your smartphone.

You'll also be reading about four teens who have had difficulties in various relationships and how DBT skills helped them develop healthier interpersonal connections. These accounts are fictional but are based on people I've worked with; the point is that their stories will help you increase your understanding of the current problems in your relationships and how these skills will help you improve the relationships in your life.

You may find that reading about these skills isn't enough. If you're having difficulty putting them into practice, do your best to ask a support person for help. If you're not comfortable speaking with your parents about these issues, think about someone else who might be willing to assist: a guidance counselor, a coach, a religious leader, another family member you trust, or a friend. People sometimes need professional therapists to help. That isn't a sign of weakness; rather, it's a sign of courage, that you're working on taking steps to better your life. Remember, the sooner you get the help you need—in whatever form it takes—the sooner you can start working on improving your relationships and your life, and feeling healthier and happier.

Speaking of which, I think it's important to point out that, while DBT was originally developed to treat severe mental health problems, these skills are really just keys to a happier, healthier way of living life. I use them on a regular basis myself, and trust me when I say that they really make a difference.

So, when you're ready, turn the page and let's get started!

Chapter 1

Looking at Yourself

For most of us, at least some of the problems we have in life are related to things we do because we've learned to behave that way. And since we've learned this behavior, the good news is that we can learn other ways of behaving that will be healthier and more effective for us. The bad news, of course, is that this takes time, energy, and a lot of hard work—but if you put this effort in, you're very likely to see some positive changes.

Increasing Your Self-Awareness

To get you started on learning these new behaviors, you'll first be asked to engage in some exercises and do some thinking about what the problems might be in your relationships: what are some of the behaviors you're engaging in that are causing you problems? You might know at least part of the answer to this question already; if so, good for you—you're ahead of the game. But even if that's the case, you'll still want to practice these exercises because you might come to some new insights about yourself, and because these exercises will also be helpful in other ways as we move on. If you don't yet have much awareness of your problem behaviors, keep in mind that taking an objective, honest look at yourself can be quite difficult, and sometimes even painful; nevertheless, this is where you need to start if you want to make positive changes in your life.

Before you can take steps to make any kind of changes, you first have to identify what it is that needs to be changed. I'm going to make this as easy for you as I can, and we'll soon look at a specific skill called *mindfulness*—which involves being fully aware and accepting of what's happening in the present moment—that will help you increase your awareness of yourself. But first, let's look at the opposite behavior, which many of us often do: *mindlessness*, or not paying attention to your surroundings or what you are experiencing.

Avoid Acting Mindlessly

Most of us have a tendency to go through life living in the past and the future, rather than in the present. Think about this for a moment: When you're getting ready for school in the morning, are you really thinking about what you're doing? Showering, brushing your teeth, doing your hair, getting dressed, and having breakfast… If you really think about it, you'll probably see that, for the most part, you're not actually thinking about those activities, but instead about what happened at school yesterday, or the party on the weekend, or the fight you had with your best friend last night, or the test you have after lunch today, or the fact that homecoming is this weekend.

Thinking about the past isn't always bad—for example, if you're recalling the nice memories of the way you and your boyfriend spent last Saturday at the park or the camping trip you took with your family last summer. But usually when we're thinking about the past, we're not thinking about the happy memories—instead, we tend to go to the unhappy, painful events that have happened in our lives. And when we do this, we trigger the painful emotions that go along with those events: we feel sad, angry, guilty, ashamed, disappointed, and so on.

Likewise with the future: Sometimes you might daydream about how you'll spend the summer when school's over or about all the opportunities and choices you'll have when you graduate. But more often, the tendency is to create a painful scenario in your head and then live in that imaginary future as though it were already happening—and this, too, triggers emotional pain, usually in the form of anxiety and worry.

Take a moment to think about how this might apply to your own life: Do you spend a lot of time thinking about the past or the future? Or both? Or do you live in the present much of the time, focusing on what you're doing in the here and now? These typical scenarios may help you respond honestly:

- When you're driving to school or sitting on the bus, are you really focusing on that drive—noticing the cars around you and paying attention to everything you need to do to safely maneuver your car; or sitting on the bus, paying attention to the other students or noticing the scenery and the houses on your route to school? Or are you thinking about what you'll be doing this weekend instead?

- If you have an argument with your parents, are you really focusing on the present moment and what's being said? Or are you also thinking that the last time you asked if you could go to a party with your best friend they also said no, and they never let you do anything and they never trust you…and so on?

- When you're at your dance or karate class, or at softball or cheerleading practice, are you really focusing on what you're doing and learning, or are you busy worrying about what will happen if you miss a step or don't kick properly or miss the ball or fall—and what others will think about you if that happens?

- While you're studying for a test, are you really focusing on that task, or are you thinking about the last test you took and how poorly you did? Or thinking about what will happen if you don't get a good grade: people will make fun of you; you won't get the straight As you were aiming for; you won't get into your first choice of colleges; there's no way you'll get into medical school …?

These are just a few everyday examples of how we tend to be mindless: going through life on automatic pilot, not really focusing on what we're doing, thinking about the past and future rather than the present moment.

There's another part of being mindful that is just as important, but for most of us is even harder than being focused on the present moment, and that's being accepting of whatever we happen to find in the present moment. So think about this: When you're sitting on the school bus noticing the kids around you, are you just noticing them, accepting them as they are, or are you judging them? Thinking to yourself, perhaps, that they're mean or pretty or weird or nerds or cool, or that they shouldn't be acting the way they are...you get the picture. While we'll be talking much further about judgments in chapter 6, for now it's important for you to know that *acceptance*—being nonjudgmental—is also part of being mindful.

Being Mindful

So we've kind of been talking around mindfulness, but what is it exactly? Mindfulness is doing one thing at a time, in the present moment, with your full attention, and with acceptance. It's focusing on what you're doing as you're doing it, and bringing a curious, accepting, nonjudgmental attitude toward whatever your experience is in that moment.

Right this second, think about what you're doing: you're reading this book. Are you doing anything else while you're reading? Are you listening to music or the television in the background? Are you petting your dog, texting your friend, or checking your Facebook page? If you are, you're not being mindful—doing *one* thing at a time in the present moment, with your *full* attention; rather, you're dividing your attention between two (or more!) activities.

Let's say you *are* just reading this book right now. Are you accepting whatever your experience is in this moment? Are you judging this book? Perhaps your mom bought it for you and you're reading it only because she's making you. If that's the case, you might be thinking that reading this book is a waste of your time—that it's boring or stupid. Or maybe, as you're trying to read, you keep getting interrupted—you're babysitting your little brother and he wants you to get him a snack or play with him, and you're judging him as annoying or thinking he shouldn't be bothering you while you're trying to read. If you're engaging in this kind of judgmental thinking, you're not being mindful.

If you're reading this book and only reading this book (so if your friend texts you, you turn your attention from the book to the text, and then bring your full attention back to reading); and if you're practicing acceptance with whatever you happen to become aware of (for example, if you notice you're feeling sad or anxious about some of the things you're reading, you just notice this rather than judging yourself for it), then you're being mindful. Here are some other examples of ways you can be mindful:

- Listening to music, and *only* listening. Not listening to music while you're Facebooking or watching television or doing your homework. And while you're only listening to music, just noticing whatever happens to come into your awareness (and keeping in mind that one of the things you need to do to improve your relationships is to increase your self-awareness), paying attention to any emotions, memories, or thoughts that might arise. Or perhaps your mom calls you to come set the table or the doorbell rings: not judging these interruptions or the people interrupting you, simply noticing them, as well as any emotions these interruptions might trigger for you—for example, thinking, *I'm feeling annoyed at being interrupted.*

- Watching your favorite television show, and *only* watching that show, not doing two or more things at once. And while you're doing this, not judging whatever is going on in the present moment: If something on the show happens that you don't like, noticing you don't like it, not that it is stupid or shouldn't have happened. Not judging the commercials you're stuck watching because your DVR broke; not judging your younger sister who's talking loudly on the telephone in the next room.

- Doing your homework, and *only* doing your homework, rather than dividing your attention between your homework and the telephone conversation you're having with your best friend. And while you're only doing your homework, not judging your teacher for giving you such a tough assignment and not judging yourself for having difficulties with it.

Mindfulness can be a really tough skill to practice, but hopefully you're starting to see how helpful it can be. In case you're not, let's take a look at some of the other ways mindfulness can be helpful.

Reducing Emotional Pain by Focusing on the Present

Living in the present has the effect of reducing the amount of emotional pain (anger, anxiety, sadness, embarrassment, and so on) in our lives; although the present can be painful as well, when we're being mindful we only have to deal with the pain of the present, rather than the pain of the present, the past, and the future all at the same time.

Reducing Emotional Pain Through Acceptance

Mindfulness also helps us increase our self-awareness. Think about it: if you're focusing on the present moment more often, you're going to be more aware of what's happening as it happens. This means you'll be able to learn about what's happening that's problematic in your relationships. You might notice that you're not paying attention to people or that your judgments of them or of yourself are getting in the way of your relationships, or you might notice that you're anxious a lot of the time and that you're allowing the anxiety to prevent you from doing things that could lead to positive relationships. There are lots of things you might become aware of, and we'll look further at these in the next chapter.

For now, let's get you practicing mindfulness so that you can learn to be more present and accepting, which will move you further in the direction of positive change.

Bringing a Sense of Balance to Your Life

By focusing on the present and on being nonjudgmental, mindfulness helps us get to a more balanced state of being, known as *equanimity*. In other words, when you're practicing mindfulness more often, you'll feel more balanced, calm, and at peace with yourself and the world around you. You might not like that something has happened, but you won't freak out about it—you'll remain equanimous, able to think about it from an objective perspective, rather than reacting from your emotional experience in that moment. We'll look at skills to help you develop this sense of wisdom further in chapter 3, but it's important for you to be aware that this is a big part of being mindful, and it will come with practice. The key, of course, is just that: practice.

Now that you hopefully understand more about how mindfulness is going to help you, let's starting talking about how to do it.

How to Practice Mindfulness

Mindfulness is great because it's so helpful in many different ways, and also because you can practice it in an infinite number of ways. Anything you do, you can do mindfully: eating, playing video games, sitting in class, taking a shower, talking to your friends, walking your dog, and so on. To bring mindfulness to your everyday activities, follow these four steps:

1. Decide what you're going to do mindfully—brush your teeth, set the table for dinner, listen to your math teacher, read a book, skateboard, breathe, or anything else you choose to focus on.

2. Start to focus: do whatever activity you've chosen, and as best as you can, bring your full attention to that activity.

3. Notice when your attention wanders. And it will wander; that's inevitable. *What's for lunch today? How did I do on the English test? What am I going to do this weekend? I wonder if Mom and Dad will let me go to Jenny's for the weekend?* And on and on...this is completely normal. Just notice when it happens.

4. Without judging yourself, the thoughts you're experiencing, the emotions that are coming up, or the interruptions that are happening, simply direct your attention back to the activity you've chosen to focus on.

You'll probably have to bring your attention back again and again to the activity you're doing mindfully, and that's okay—it's pretty normal, especially when you first start practicing. Don't get frustrated; it will get easier. But make sure you keep practicing. As with any new skill, that's how it will start to come more naturally.

Breathing Mindfully

So far the kind of mindfulness exercises we've been talking about involve bringing mindfulness to anything you might be doing in your daily life—these are known as *informal* mindfulness exercises. But there are other ways of practicing mindfulness, known as *formal* practices, where you have to set aside a certain amount of time to practice, rather than just bringing mindfulness to your current experience. One such practice, and the most helpful one to start with, is a breathing exercise. Take your time as you read the following exercise.

Exercise: Mindful Breathing

Turning your attention to your breath, begin to notice how it feels to breathe. Notice the feel of the cool air as it flows in through your nose. Notice your stomach expanding as your lungs fill with air. Observe your stomach rising and falling, and your chest rising and falling, as you slowly inhale and exhale. As you continue to breathe, allow yourself to become aware of any sensations as you focus on your breath. Notice the pace of your breathing; notice whether you're breathing shallowly or deeply. How does it feel? Is it comfortable? As best as you can, don't judge whatever your experience is. Just continue to pay attention to it—just observe it.

As you continue to observe, you'll probably notice that your attention wanders—perhaps a noise outside catches your attention and you start to wonder who's walking by the house; maybe you notice you're hungry or thirsty; or you might be thinking you have better things to do with your time. Whatever thoughts arise, just notice them without judging, and return your attention to your breath. You may have to do this over and over again—that's okay. Your attention will likely wander a lot. Notice any frustration, anxiety, boredom, or other emotions, and don't judge them—just observe them.

Some people become aware of feelings of relaxation; this is sometimes a nice side effect of practicing mindfulness—of doing just one thing in the present moment and practicing acceptance. If you can sit with this breathing exercise for a couple of minutes, go ahead and keep focusing on your breathing; if it feels too long already, you can stop focusing on your breathing (but by all means, please continue to breathe!) and continue reading.

Practicing Mindfulness on Your Own

Knowing about mindfulness isn't going to get you anywhere; you have to put this and all of the other skills we'll be talking about into practice. The more you practice, the more positive changes you'll see in yourself. Among other things, your self-awareness will increase, and you'll probably notice your ability to manage your emotions improves—in other words, you'll be less reactive to things and able to make healthier choices. But how to practice?

Formal or Informal?

It's important to practice both formal and informal mindfulness exercises. For many people, it's easier to practice only informal mindfulness exercises because we lead such busy lives and it's often hard to make time to fit in new things; in informal practices we don't have to find time to practice—we can just do it as we're doing the things we need to do anyway. However, in the mental health profession, we do see differences between people who practice only informally and those who practice both formally and informally: positive changes happen more quickly for those who practice formal exercises regularly and frequently. So while it might be easier to do just informal mindfulness exercises, if you want to make positive changes in your life, I strongly suggest you make a commitment to yourself to find the time to do both kinds of practices on a regular basis.

We've already talked about the kinds of activities you can practice informal mindfulness with—there are literally an infinite number of ways to practice, as anything you're doing you can do mindfully. In addition, we've looked at a mindful breathing exercise. Throughout this book, we'll look at other ways of practicing formally, so be sure to incorporate these other exercises into your daily practice as we go along.

Where to Practice

With informal exercises, of course, you'll be practicing wherever you happen to be; with formal exercises, it will be easier for you to practice, especially as you begin, if you're in a quiet place where interruptions might be minimal—in your bedroom, or another quiet room in the house if you share a room; in the backyard; or in the library. A quiet place isn't necessary; if one isn't available, it just means you'll have more interruptions and distractions to notice. So just because it isn't quiet and peaceful doesn't mean you can't practice on the bus, or in the backseat of the car, or in study hall; you just might find it a little more challenging!

How Long to Practice

I encourage people to start off with shorter practices, whether it's a formal or an informal activity; otherwise it can get somewhat frustrating as you find yourself more and more distracted as time goes on. So if you choose to practice informally while you're doing your homework, practice for two minutes, then five, then ten, and so on. Or if you're walking the dog, choose a fairly short part of your route that you'll walk mindfully. With formal exercises, likewise, it will be helpful to start off with shorter periods of time—again, two to five minutes—and then gradually increase your practice.

Eyes Open or Closed?

Mindfulness experts have different opinions on this question. I like to be flexible, so here's my suggestion: if you have to close your eyes in order to stay focused, then close your eyes. However, you want to be able to practice mindfulness wherever and whenever you can, and you might feel kind of weird sitting on the bus with your eyes closed. The overall goal with mindfulness is for us to live our lives more mindfully, and it's hard to go through life with our eyes closed! So as much as you can, practice with your eyes open.

Your Next Steps

Over the next week or so, be sure to practice formal and informal exercises as often as possible. Schedule some time to do formal practices such as the breathing exercise you did earlier. Bringing mindfulness informally to activities you're doing throughout the day is also important, so do this as often as you think of it. You may want to do things to help you make a point of remembering, like putting a reminder in your smartphone or daily planner.

In addition, you need to put your mindfulness skills into practice in interactions with other people in order to increase your self-awareness. So when you're talking to your parents, a teacher, your boyfriend or girlfriend, or your closest friend, do your best to really pay attention to what's happening in the moment instead of trying to figure out what you're going to say next; or worrying what the other person is thinking about you; or wondering if you're coming across as awkward, and so on. Focus on the conversation, and work on increasing your awareness of yourself in that conversation: notice your facial expression, body language, and tone of voice; be aware of your emotions as they come and go; and see if you can pick up on the other person's responses to you as you speak.

As best you can, remember not to judge yourself for what thoughts, physical sensations, or emotions you may find yourself noticing as you practice—you may not like it, but that's where other skills will come in to help you change. And the only way to make the changes is to first shine a light on what's interfering with your ability to be effective in your interactions with others. It may be painful, but remember: short-term pain for long-term gain!

In the next chapter, we'll continue to put these mindfulness skills into practice to help you identify what's going on for you that may be contributing to your relationship problems. We'll look at some examples of things that contribute to difficulties in relationships, and you'll read about some teens, the problems they're having, and how they're using these skills to make positive changes in their lives.

Chapter 2

Looking at Your Relationships

So how have you done so far? Are you paying attention to yourself? Are you noticing things that might be getting in the way of having the relationships you'd like? Especially if you've been practicing the skill of being mindful that you learned in chapter 1, you may have gained some insight into and awareness of what's preventing you from being effective in your relationships; but if you haven't had any aha moments yet, don't worry—in this chapter we're going to take a closer look at what some of those problems might be. Hopefully you'll be able to relate to some of the issues you read about here, and will come to see how these issues can get in the way of healthy relationships.

Relationships: Healthy or Unhealthy?

When you think about how you'd like your relationships to be, what comes to mind? I think the defining word for me is "balance," which for many things is almost synonymous with "healthy." So let's take a closer look at what we mean when we say we want our relationships to be balanced, or healthy. Along the way, you'll meet some teens who have a variety of problems in their relationships.

Communication

In any relationship—whether it's with your friends, your parents, your teachers, or others—communication is key. If you don't communicate properly, you'll find yourself in all sorts of trouble. Think about a time that happened to you. Perhaps you were speaking to a friend and said something she misunderstood, and she became angry with you; maybe you sent a text or e-mail that was misinterpreted and resulted in hard feelings. When you're communicating with others, it's important to be as clear and concise as possible and to check your own perceptions of what's happening in order to avoid misunderstandings. Let's look at Carter's story as an example of how ineffective communication can have negative consequences for relationships.

• Carter's Story

Carter is seventeen years old. Ever since he can remember, he's had problems with anxiety and anger, and he can become very aggressive when he's trying to get his point across. It doesn't help that he has a hard time expressing things to the people he cares about because he worries they'll become angry with him; the result is that he tends to stuff things down and ignore his emotions until a situation becomes too much for him to bear, and then he blows up. He's been known to throw things when he's angry, and Merrin, his girlfriend of two years, recently told him that if he doesn't get his anger under control, she won't want to be with him anymore. She admits to being fearful of him when he gets angry.

His anger has also affected Carter's friendships. He used to be in a band with three other guys his age; they had been playing together for about two years and were doing well, and had even done small tours the last two summers. One night the four of them got into a fight. Carter's anger got the better of him; he broke some of their equipment and said some really hurtful things to his friends related to issues he had avoided addressing, rather than talking to them before his anger and resentment built up. Carter's friends ended up telling him they wanted him out of the band, and they haven't spoken to him since. Not only did he lose his band and the equipment he broke, but he lost three good friends as well.

We'll take a closer look at how to communicate in a more balanced, assertive way in chapter 3; but for now, ask yourself: do you communicate effectively, or do you think poor communication might be getting in the way of your ability to be effective in your interactions with others?

Limit-Setting

Healthy relationships involve balanced limits, which means that you give to, as well as take from, the other person. Sometimes people get into a pattern of taking all the time—for example, expecting your best friend who just got her driver's license to drive you to school every day or your mom to have dinner ready for you the minute you get home from band practice. When you regularly count on another person to give to you, you often begin to take that person for granted. You might forget to express appreciation for what the person is doing for you, and your attitude might become one of expectation rather than gratitude. Usually, when this is the case, that person starts to feel unappreciated and resentful, which can cause problems in the relationship in the long run.

Can you think of a time when you were on the receiving end of this attitude? When you felt taken for granted by people in your life, when they seemed to just expect you to do something for them? Doesn't feel very good, does it? And that's the other side of this coin—when you're giving all the time, you'll start to resent the other person for taking, even if you're the one who made the decision to do the giving in the first place. Take a look at the following story as an example.

• Rebecca's Story

Rebecca was thirteen when her parents separated two years ago, and she's been struggling with her emotions since then. Her connections with both parents have been chaotic. They've been arguing a lot; Rebecca often feels that neither her mother nor her father understands her or even tries to, and she disobeys them frequently, which results in her being grounded and even more arguing. Now, two years later, her mom has a new boyfriend, Tom. Rebecca's having difficulty accepting Tom; her mother has always put Rebecca's needs first, and suddenly she can no longer count on that to be the case. Rebecca feels a lot of anger toward her mother and is resentful of the fact that sometimes her mom is spending time with Tom when Rebecca would like to spend time with her. Because she's feeling so angry, Rebecca's been having a hard time communicating with her mother about these issues.

It seems that Rebecca takes her mother for granted; in the opposite direction, she has a hard time setting healthy limits with her friends. She's always giving more than taking, and she often ends up feeling used by people. For example, she bought a friend a cell phone because her friend's parents wouldn't get her one; now Rebecca is stuck with a monthly bill she can't afford, and the friend no longer spends time with her. Rebecca's friends have also gotten into the habit of coming over to her house on weekends; they know they can drink and smoke there because her mom is usually at Tom's house. Rebecca worries that her mother will find out and she'll get into trouble, but she doesn't assert herself with her friends because she worries that if she does, they'll stop wanting to spend time with her.

Rebecca's story is a good example of how people get stuck in a trap of giving because they think that's what they need to do in order to make others like them. But in a healthy relationship, there's a balance of giving and taking, and neither person feels taken for granted or obligated to give. Instead, you give because you want to give, because it makes you feel good to do something for the other person. Do you think you have healthy limits, or is this something that contributes to your difficulties in getting along with others?

Self-Esteem

What exactly does it mean to have healthy self-esteem? It means feeling good about who you are and loving yourself as a person. It's about recognizing your strengths, as well as acknowledging the challenges you have and realizing that you're still a good person even if you make mistakes, do things you regret, fail a math test, disappoint your parents, and so on. It's understanding that who you are is separate from what you do, and that even though you sometimes do things that you or others may judge as bad or wrong, you can still love and respect the person you are.

It's also important to emphasize that having good self-esteem doesn't mean that you feel you're better or more deserving than others—rather, it translates into having a healthy respect for yourself and for others.

If you have poor self-esteem, it will usually be more difficult for you to connect in a healthy way with others. If you don't love yourself and see the goodness in yourself as a person, it will often be difficult for you to believe that you are deserving of healthy relationships and of the respect that comes with them. You'll probably believe that you don't deserve to be treated well and that you always have to give in order to make someone want to continue to be your friend—like Rebecca. In reality, the more you feed into these beliefs by continually giving and by staying in relationships where you're allowing others to treat you disrespectfully, the more your self-esteem will suffer.

On the flip side, some people with low self-esteem are the ones who become bullies and treat others poorly, because that makes them feel better about themselves. Michael's story is an example.

• Michael's Story

Michael is fourteen years old and has attention deficit/ hyperactivity disorder (ADHD). He's always felt that he's been treated differently by teachers in school, and he is aware that he's disrupting his class at times, but he can't seem to help himself. Over the years, his self-esteem has suffered, and he often judges himself and feels down. He has problems at home and usually doesn't get along with his parents, and that just adds to his loneliness and his feeling of being misunderstood. Michael has found, however, that he's funny, and that by using his sense of humor to pick on some of the less popular kids in school, he's been able to make some friends. His sharp tongue seems to keep his friends in line—they know that if he decides to target them, life will be miserable, at least for a while, so they do their best to stay on his good side. While Michael still doesn't feel good about himself, and in fact often feels guilt and shame for the way he treats others, at least now he has friends and doesn't feel like a loser at school anymore.

You can see from Michael's story that bullying is a way for some people to try to feel good about themselves and fit in. Just as with giving too much, though, the more you put others down to try to make yourself feel better, the more other emotions will build up (in this case, guilt and shame), and you'll end up making the situation worse. Many of the skills we'll look at throughout this book will gradually help improve the way you feel about yourself. But ask yourself now, is this something that might be getting in the way of your ability to have healthy relationships?

Depression and Anxiety

Sometimes what contributes to low self-esteem, and makes it difficult for people to have healthy friendships, is depression or anxiety. If someone is feeling depressed, she'll experience a low mood or sadness. Often her motivation to do things and her energy level decrease; she may have trouble sleeping, and she won't want to go out and socialize because she doesn't feel like it. She might feel like she doesn't have anything to say to others, and she might fear that her friends will see she's not her usual self.

If someone has anxiety, she may overthink things and begin to worry a lot. Her worry thoughts—*What if I make a fool of myself?* or *People will think I'm weird*, or *What if no one likes me?*—will often prevent her from going out and socializing with friends, or meeting new people.

Do you experience these problems? Do you find yourself feeling depressed or anxious, and notice that the thoughts associated with these feelings prevent you from doing things? Do you let these thoughts and feelings get in the way of your interactions with others? Caitlyn's story can help you get a better idea of how such problems might be affecting your relationships.

• Caitlyn's Story

Caitlyn is eighteen years old. She's been bullied all through school and at some point gave up on making friends. She's decided it's not worth it, because she can't trust people and they'll inevitably end up hurting her. Caitlyn has low self-esteem because of the bullying she's experienced, and in fact, she's developed something called social anxiety—*a fear of being in social situations—which causes her to avoid any kind of social situation as much as she can. Her worry thoughts get in the way of her even trying to meet people or make friends; for example,* They'll just end up hurting me, *or* I can't trust anyone, *or* People don't actually like me, so why bother trying? *Caitlyn has no friends, and she constantly feels sad and lonely.*

You can see from Caitlyn's story that problems with relationships (for example, being bullied, not having friends) can certainly contribute to feelings of depression or anxiety, and that depression and anxiety can feed into problems in connecting with others. Again, many of the skills we'll look at in this book will help with feelings of depression and anxiety, but if you think you're depressed or anxious—and especially if you ever have thoughts of hurting or killing yourself—it is very important that you reach out to someone who can help: a parent, an aunt or uncle, or a sibling; a teacher, coach, or guidance counselor; or even the parent of a friend. You don't have to go through these things alone, and it can help to have someone who understands what you're experiencing.

By the way, having depression or anxiety doesn't necessarily mean you have unhealthy relationships. If you have these difficulties with your mood and you have people you trust with whom you talk about these problems, you can still have healthy connections with others, although those connections may at times be negatively affected by your depression or anxiety. But if you don't have people to turn to when depression and anxiety worsen, and instead you let these emotional problems control you, they will definitely contribute to unhealthy relationships.

Lack of Social Skills

"Social skills" as a category is a little more vague than the others, and it may be more difficult for you to figure out on your own whether you're lacking in this area. One of the reasons for this difficulty is that many people feel socially awkward even though others don't perceive them that way; in other words, their self-judgment doesn't actually fit with reality. Caitlyn, for example, tries to avoid social situations as much as possible and so probably doesn't get much practice socializing; this, coupled with her anxiety and her history of being bullied, probably leads her to judge herself as socially awkward, even though to others, she might simply seem somewhat shy or standoffish.

Some people, however, truly haven't developed the skills most people have in terms of interacting with others. Sometimes this is related to a mental health problem (for example, severe anxiety or even a mild form of autism); often it's less serious, and related to factors like poor self-esteem or a lack of practice or opportunities to learn how to be appropriate and comfortable in social situations.

So what do we mean by social skills, exactly? People who are lacking social skills or who are socially awkward often say things or behave in ways that are considered inappropriate by the people they're interacting with. They may crack jokes that seem tasteless to others or laugh at things that others don't find funny; they may bring up subjects that don't seem appropriate given the people they're speaking with; they may spill their guts about all their problems to people they don't know very well. People lacking in social skills often don't pick up on the social cues being given to them by others, such as body language and facial expressions—for example, they may stand too close to others when they're speaking; not pick up on someone else's discomfort regarding a certain topic as other people might, which would likely lead to a change in subject; or regularly interrupt others while they're speaking, and so on.

Again, because whether you're socially awkward is something that's often difficult to determine on your own (either because you're overly sensitive about it and your self-judgments cause you to think you're socially awkward when you're not; or because you simply have no awareness that you indeed do have difficulties in this area), it's a good idea to check it out with someone you trust. Explain to a parent, sibling, friend, relative, coach, teacher, or someone else you trust that you're trying to learn skills to help you improve the relationships in your life, and ask if that person can give you any feedback about why you might have troubles in this area. Does she see you make mistakes she can point out for you to learn from? Knowing you in whatever way she does, is there any advice she can give you that might help you improve your social skills? You can also ask her to give you feedback if she notices problematic things you're doing as you interact with her. And try to remember to not judge yourself if this is an issue. Instead, congratulate yourself for your openness in discovering at least part of the problem, so that you can begin to work to change it.

Variety of Relationships

Something else that contributes to the health of relationships is the variety of personal connections you have in your life. Some people don't have anyone they would consider a friend, often because depression, anxiety, or low-self-esteem has prevented them from putting themselves in situations where they could meet people with whom they might develop friendships. If you don't have many friends in your life, you'll be more reliant on the family or friends you do have, which can take a toll on those people. The more people you have in your life, the less you have to rely on any one person, and the healthier the relationships you have will be—you won't have the same tendency to take any one person for granted, but instead will value the time you spend together.

Do you ever notice that you have people in your life who get on your nerves? That when you spend too much time with them you start to annoy each other? That's a good sign that you need a break from those people—but it's hard to take a break from one person if you don't have others in your life with whom you can spend time. Connecting with others is very important to us as human beings, and isolation actually has negative consequences—not only for our emotional health, but also for our physical health. So consider the relationships you have in your life currently—not just how healthy or balanced they are, but the number of them. Do you have enough to satisfy you in your life? In fact, it's not a bad idea to actually list the people you have in your life in each of these categories:

- Family supports (family members you rely on and know you can turn to for support when needed)

- Close friends (friends you can count on and confide in)

- Social friends (friends you may not be very close with, but with whom you do social activities and whose company you enjoy)

- Mentors (people you look up to, role models; for example, coaches, teachers, family members)

- Community supports (for example, religious leaders, teachers, coaches, or leaders of groups you belong to)

Don't worry if you repeat some names in certain categories; this list is simply meant to help you assess the relationships you have in your life. Also, remember that everyone has different needs socially, so your list might not look the same as a list your best friend or your sister might make. What you need to keep in mind, however, is that if you don't have enough people in your life (whatever "enough" looks like for *you*), the relationships you do have will suffer, and so will your emotional and physical health.

Hopefully you've been thinking about how much—or how little—weaknesses in these areas might be contributing to your relationship difficulties. As you can see from the teens you've met in this chapter, people often have more than one of these difficulties, and that makes having healthy relationships extra challenging. To help you further identify what problems in your life might be holding you back from being the person you'd like to be in relationships, make sure you're putting the techniques and skills in this book into practice. Working your way through this book while practicing the ideas you're learning is the best way to get the most out of this experience.

Applying Mindfulness to Your Relationships

Once you've been practicing mindfulness for a while and are starting to get the hang of it, you can begin to bring mindfulness to help even more with the question of the problems in your relationships. This is a bit of formal and informal practice put together. Following are some guidelines to help:

- Choose an interaction to practice with; having a conversation with your parent or sibling, or with a good friend, is usually a nice, casual way to start.

- While you're interacting with the other person, notice your own physical sensations, emotions, and thoughts. Be mindful of your body language (for example, are your arms crossed or your fists clenched? What's the expression on your face?) and the words you're using to communicate, as well as the tone and volume of your voice.

- Pay attention to the other person's responses to you—her body language and facial expression as well as the words she's using to communicate with you, her tone of voice, and so on.

Because this practice takes a lot of concentration, it can be helpful if you first choose someone who knows about the work you're doing on yourself. You could even tell her you're doing an experiment and ask for her assistance, so that after the interaction you can compare notes: What did you observe in her, and what was her actual reaction? And what did she observe in you during the interaction? Getting this kind of objective feedback can be invaluable, so much so that you may even want to take this one step further and make a video recording of the interaction so that you can see for yourself what happened: How did you look, what did you sound like, and what was the message conveyed? Did you notice things about the person, in reviewing the video, that you hadn't noticed during the interaction? If you don't have anyone you trust with whom you can be open about an exercise like this, just do your best to use your new skills to remain in the present moment and accepting while interacting with others. Remember, the goal right now is just to become aware of anything that may be hindering your ability to have healthy relationships with others, so pay attention!

Your Next Steps

Since slow and easy does it, your practice for this chapter in addition to the exercise just outlined is simply to continue doing the same things you've been doing since chapter 1: practicing mindfulness formally and informally, becoming aware and accepting of whatever you happen to notice about what's getting in the way of healthy relationships for you.

As you interact with others, it's important to continue to observe yourself. Notice as best as you can what your experience is during interactions, and what things are preventing you from interacting effectively. Here are some questions to think about in order to identify the problems in your life that are getting in the way of relationships:

- Are you expressing yourself clearly and getting your point across?

- Are you shutting the other person down in conversation by being interruptive, judgmental, blaming, or negative in other ways?

- Do you have a tendency to give more than you take in a relationship and then end up feeling resentful of the other person for taking advantage of you or using you?

- Or do you have a tendency to take more than you give in a relationship, so that the other person expresses feeling taken for granted and unappreciated?

- Are you judgmental of yourself?

- Do you feel unworthy of being treated respectfully in a relationship?

- Do you worry that if you try to be more assertive about getting your needs met in a relationship the other person will no longer want to be friends with you?

- Are you feeling anxious or depressed?

- Are you experiencing worry thoughts or making assumptions about how the other person is going to respond?

- Do you feel—or have you been told—that you're socially awkward, not picking up on social cues the way others seem to?

- Do you feel as though you don't have enough relationships in your life?

It's important that you have at least some ideas about what the problems might be—ineffective communication, unhealthy limits, low self-esteem, depression or anxiety, problems picking up on social cues, or a lack of relationships—before you move on to the next chapter, where we'll begin looking at some other skills to help you improve in these areas. So if you're still unsure about what's preventing you from having fulfilling relationships, spend some time really thinking about these questions. Practice lots of mindfulness. If you can, ask a person you trust for input. And remember, although some of these things may be difficult to acknowledge within yourself, and to hear from someone else, identifying the problems you face is the first step in changing them.

Chapter 3

How to Get What You Want (More Often!)

Because communication is such a big part of relating to others successfully, and often causes such problems for people when they're interacting with others, we're going to look at this area next. In this chapter, we'll look at four different ways of communicating. You'll have an opportunity to assess your own communication style, and then we'll look more closely at the healthiest, most balanced way of communicating. As we do this, though, remember that you need to continue practicing mindfulness and developing your self-awareness regarding the way you interact with others.

Communication Styles

The way you speak with people has a direct effect on what your relationship will be like with them, and this point is important whether you're talking to a rep at your cell phone company or to your dad. Either way, you need to remember that the words you use, your tone of voice, your attitude, and so on will influence whether that person wants to give you what you're asking for or help you get your needs met. For example, when Rebecca tries to talk to her mom about the fact that she's feeling abandoned, her anger takes over and she ends up yelling and being verbally abusive toward her mom. I don't know about you, but when someone yells at me and calls me names, I don't usually feel very motivated to help that person; instead, I feel hurt and angry and I just want to get away from him.

Some people go in the opposite direction. Rather than becoming abusive, they stuff their emotions and don't express them at all. The problem with this is that the person suppressing his emotions still doesn't get his needs met, which can result in feelings of resentment that will also have negative consequences for the relationship; over time resentment continues to build, and it usually gets to a point where, like Carter, the person can't continue suppressing emotion and instead explodes. This could result in his ending the relationship rather than trying to fix it, or even in the other person ending the friendship rather than continuing to be involved with someone who's going to treat him this way.

These are just a couple of ways that poor communication skills can have negative consequences for your relationships with others. Next, let's take a look at the four different ways of communicating—the first three being not so healthy, and the fourth being the one to aim for.

Passive Communication

Someone who is *passive* in the way he communicates doesn't often express feelings, opinions, or beliefs, usually out of a fear that he'll rock the boat or cause problems in the relationship. For the passive person, the goal is to avoid conflict. The person who won't give an opinion as to which movie he'd like to see, or where he'd like to have dinner, is a passive communicator.

The problem for the passive person is that not speaking up about what he wants often means he doesn't get his needs met. Over time, not speaking up also leads others to expect that he will go along with what they want to do, or that he'll do as they ask, because he always has in the past. As the relationship progresses in this way and the passive person continues to not get his needs met, he'll likely begin to feel resentful, even though he's made the choice to not express his wants and needs.

Passive-Aggressive Communication

The person who uses sarcasm and eye-rolling instead of expressing himself directly, who slams doors, and who gives others the silent treatment is a *passive-aggressive* communicator. He's trying to communicate his wants or emotions, but instead of doing this in a clear manner, he does so in an aggressive but underhanded way. Like passive communicators, people who are passive-aggressive are usually trying to avoid conflict, but the behaviors they engage in can often be even more damaging than just saying outright what they'd really like. For example, you're going out with a couple of friends to see a movie; you'd really like to see a horror movie but your other two friends want to see an action film. You tell them you don't mind (passive), but inside you're feeling angry and as if they ganged up on you, preventing you from seeing the movie you really wanted to see. So you get up multiple times during the movie, purposely being disruptive (aggressive). After all, if you don't get to enjoy yourself, why should they?

As you can hopefully see, passive-aggressive communication is unhealthy. It can be very damaging to your friendships, as the people in your life will likely not appreciate the underhanded behavior. And you still face the same problem of not getting your needs met, and feeling your resentment build. Sooner or later, either you or your friends are going to blow up in this kind of relationship.

Aggressive Communication

You may have heard the saying "It's my way or the highway." Someone who says such things or behaves in this way is *aggressive*—he wants to get his own way, and he may bully others in order to get it. An aggressive communicator is controlling, threatening, and sometimes even verbally or otherwise abusive. The bottom line is that he'll do pretty much whatever he has to in order to get his needs met, and he doesn't care so much whether you get what you want.

The obvious problem with being an aggressive communicator is that most people won't put up with that kind of treatment for very long. At some point, they'll decide that they don't deserve or want to be treated so disrespectfully, and they'll end the relationship. An additional problem that can arise for the aggressive communicator is that his aggression can sometimes trigger in him feelings of guilt and shame, as he might recognize that he's treating people in abusive or unfair ways—remember Michael, for example, the bully you met in the last chapter.

Assertive Communication

The last communication style, which is healthy and balanced, is *assertive*. Someone who is assertive communicates clearly and concisely—he states his opinion or talks about his feelings in a way that is respectful of himself and the other person. While his goal is often to get his own needs met, the assertive person is also concerned about other people getting their needs met, and so he's the person who will try to negotiate or compromise. For example, maybe one of your friends wants to go see an action film, but he's willing to come back to the movies with you on Tuesday night to see the horror movie you had your heart set on.

We'll be talking a lot more about assertiveness and how to be assertive shortly, so we'll leave it at that for now. The next thing for you to do is consider what communication style you yourself tend to use most often.

What's Your Communication Style?

Whenever we communicate, the style we use is going to depend on many things, like who we're communicating with, what the situation is, and what our state of mind is at that time. But most of us tend to use one or two styles in most interactions. That said, the following quiz isn't about labeling you; it's intended to help you get an idea of what style you tend to use most often.

Communication Styles Quiz

Read each of these statements, and check the ones that you feel apply to you *more often than not*. Add up the check marks in each section to get an idea of what communication style you tend to use most often.

Passive

_____ I try to push my feelings away rather than express them to others.

_____ I worry that expressing myself will cause others to be angry with me or to not like me.

_____ I say "I don't care" or "It doesn't matter to me" when I do care and it actually does matter.

_____ I keep quiet because I don't want to upset others.

_____ I go along with others' opinions because I don't want to be different.

Total: _____

Passive-Aggressive

_____ I have a tendency to be sarcastic when having conversations with others.

_____ I tend to give people the silent treatment when I'm angry with them.

_____ I find myself saying one thing, but really thinking another thing (for example, going along with someone else's idea because she's the most popular person in the group, but really wishing I was doing something else).

_____ I'm reluctant to express my emotions in words, and so I find that how I feel gets expressed in other ways (like slamming doors, or other aggressive behaviors).

_____ I worry that expressing myself will cause others to be angry with me, or to stop liking me, so I try to get my message across in more subtle ways.

Total: _____

Aggressive

_____ I'm concerned with getting my own way, regardless of how it affects others.

_____ I yell, curse, or use other aggressive means of asserting myself.

_____ I get the sense that my friends fear me.

_____ I find myself not really caring whether others get what they need as long as my needs are met. This sometimes makes me disrespectful toward others when communicating with them.

_____ I have an "It's my way or the highway" attitude.

Total: _____

Assertive

_____ I believe that I have a right to express my own opinions and emotions.

_____ When I'm having a disagreement with someone, I express my opinions and emotions clearly and honestly.

_____ When I'm communicating with others, I treat them with respect, while also respecting myself.

_____ I listen closely to what the other person is saying, sending the message that I'm trying to understand that person's perspective.

_____ I try to negotiate with the other person if we both have different goals, rather than being focused on getting my own needs met.

Total: _____

In which category did you score the highest? Was this what you expected?

Communication Styles Are Learned

We all learn how to communicate from somewhere. The biggest influence usually comes from our families as we grow up. Think about the communication styles of your family members: do they tend to be more passive, passive-aggressive, aggressive, or assertive? If you've grown up seeing one family member give the others the silent treatment whenever he becomes angry with them, you might have learned that that's how to behave when you feel angry. Or you might dislike that experience enough that you've learned to behave in other ways when you become angry—perhaps you become aggressive and shout it out, or you become assertive and are able to calmly discuss your feelings of anger.

When you're looking at your patterns and where you learned them from, the goal is not to blame your family for your problems. But if you recognize that certain patterns have developed because you've learned them from someone, it can help you change those patterns and start to develop healthier ones, which leads us to the idea of how to change your current communication style so that you're communicating more assertively on a regular basis.

Assertiveness

Assertiveness is a gigantic topic, but I'll do my best to cover the basics for you here. If you decide that you really have difficulty being assertive, you may want to look into taking a class on assertiveness, or joining a support group. Have patience with yourself, though, because it usually takes lots of time and practice to change the patterns you've been stuck in for most of your life.

Remembering that you have to increase your awareness of something before you can change it, start by using your mindfulness skills to help you notice when you're not being assertive. For example, you might notice that you're starting to feel an uncomfortable emotion; tuning in to this, you may find you're starting to feel resentful because you're not speaking up about your preference in a situation.

Assertiveness is also connected to self-esteem. If you don't feel good about who you are as a person, it's more difficult to be assertive because you may not feel like you deserve what you're asking for. However, it also works the other way: the more you assert yourself, the more you'll increase your self-esteem, so don't give up on assertiveness just because you think it's doomed from the start!

Asserting yourself is a healthy way of living your life. You have the right to express your emotions, opinions, and beliefs—and of course, others have the right to disagree with your opinions and beliefs!

For the purposes of this section of the book, we'll be looking at assertiveness only as it applies in two types of situations. The first is when you're asking someone for something. For example, you ask your parents if you can go to a friend's cottage this weekend, or you ask your sister to give you extra time on the family computer tonight because you've got an assignment due tomorrow. In these situations, someone has something you want, and assertiveness will increase your chances of getting it.

The second type of situation is when someone asks you for something, and you want to say no to that request. Saying no can be difficult—again, if you have low self-esteem you may not feel that you deserve to say no, or you may feel obligated to say yes because of who is making the request. You may not feel you're able to say no to a teacher, for example, because he has a degree of power over you. Sometimes you might worry that if you say no to a friend he'll be angry with you or decide not to be your friend anymore (a concern also related to low self-esteem). Tied into this, you might be a person who avoids conflict at all costs, and so you feel you can't say no because that might lead to an argument. Sometimes people just feel guilty for saying no, and so they say yes to avoid feeling an uncomfortable emotion.

Whether you're making a request of someone or saying no to someone else's request, being assertive means communicating your emotions, thoughts, and beliefs in a way that's clear, but also respectful to both you and the other person. It involves caring about the other person and his needs, which means that negotiation and compromise often come into play as you try to get your own needs met, as well as to meet the needs of the other person. Here are some guidelines to help you increase your assertive communication.

Be Clear About Your Goals

Often what gets in the way of people getting what they want is their own indecisiveness—they're not entirely clear on what their goals are. If you're not clear on what you want in a situation, how on earth can you expect the other person to be clear about it? In an interpersonal situation, our primary goals might relate to three areas: the outcome, the relationship, or our own self-respect.

Outcome

When your priority in a situation is to get something from someone (for example, to borrow money from your parents), or to say no to another person's request (for example, to skip a concert your boyfriend wants you to go to), your goal relates to the outcome. In other words, your main concern is getting what you want, or saying no to what someone else wants.

Relationship

So what you want in the situation is to borrow some money from your parents, or maybe to tell your boyfriend you don't want to go to the concert he's asked you to—you have an outcome you'd like to achieve. But maybe in this situation, you're less concerned with whether you get what you want, and more concerned with maintaining your connection with the others involved. If so, your goal here relates to the relationship.

Self-Respect

Maybe you'd like to get your needs met, but what's even more important to you in the situations you find yourself in is that you feel good about yourself for the way you interacted when all is said and done. Even if you don't actually get your needs met (your parents won't lend you money, or your boyfriend isn't taking no for an answer because he's already bought the concert tickets), as long as you come out of the situation feeling good about yourself for the way you behaved, you've met your goal—even if a relationship has to change or end as a result.

One final note here about self-respect, since it's obviously a pretty important goal that we want to work on as often as possible. In an ideal world, you'd feel good about yourself every time you engage with others, but unfortunately it doesn't always work that way. Sometimes you might choose to sacrifice self-respect a bit for the sake of the outcome or the relationship.

Let's take a look at an example: We know that Rebecca and her mother have really been struggling to get along with each other, and that Rebecca, at least, is now trying really hard to change this. Early one Saturday morning, Rebecca's mother comes to her bedroom door and asks Rebecca to go grocery shopping with her. This is certainly not something Rebecca feels like getting up early for on a Saturday morning! But knowing how rocky things have been with her mom lately, Rebecca doesn't feel like she can say no to this request. Her goal here is to continue to improve her relationship with her mother, and that means, in this instance, sacrificing a bit of her self-respect, as she does what her mother asks instead of sleeping in as she herself wants to.

Obviously Rebecca isn't behaving toward her mother in a way that she'll later regret, but there is a part of her that likely is wishing she didn't have to give in to this request, and that she could be more assertive; in this way, her self-respect will suffer a little. If Rebecca made these kinds of choices on a regular basis, this would become a problem and her self-respect would begin to decrease. But there's likely also a part of Rebecca that feels good about making the choice to help her mother on this occasion, which helps us see that this issue is not cut-and-dried! The bottom line is, the more you can behave in ways that don't reduce your self-respect, the better; but sometimes you may find you have to sacrifice self-respect—hopefully just in small ways, as in Rebecca's example—in order to achieve the outcome you want or to improve your connection with another person.

Keeping these three possible goal areas in mind, it's important to figure out which one is most important to you in any given situation. Sometimes, we run into an ideal situation where it is possible to reach our goals in all three areas—we get what we want (or say no), we maintain a good relationship with the other person, and we feel good about ourselves for our behavior. But unfortunately, you might more often find yourself in situations where it's not possible to come out meeting all three of these goals. When this happens, you need to be clear in your own mind about what's most important for you in that situation: to get what you're asking for or to stick to your no, to preserve the relationship, or to respect yourself after the interaction. Keeping this in the front of your mind as you proceed with the interaction, try to act in ways that will make it more likely that you'll achieve this result.

How to Be Assertive

Now that you've decided what goal area you'll be focusing on in the situation, you can use the method I'll outline in this section to help you communicate assertively. Unfortunately, these steps don't come with guarantees—when you're dealing with another person, you might not get what you want no matter how skillfully you act. Using these steps, though, will make it more likely you'll reach your goals.

I'll run through the steps first, and then we'll look at some examples to help you understand more fully how to apply them.

Describe the situation.

When you're being assertive, it's very helpful to describe, factually, the situation you're referring to so that everyone's clear on what's being discussed. It's also important to pay close attention to the language you're using. We'll talk more about this in chapter 6; for now, as best as you can, stick to factual, descriptive language rather than using judgments.

State your opinion and emotions.

Without blaming or judging, tell the other person your thoughts, and, if applicable, your emotions about the situation you've just described.

Clearly state what you want.

This is where you get very specific about what you're asking for (or, in the case of someone else's request, that you're saying no). Don't be shy—come out and say it! And make sure your request is clear—people often make an observation and then expect the other person to read their minds about what they would like. For example, your mom might mention, "There are a lot of dishes to be done tonight and it's late." From this statement, you might surmise that she's asking you to help with the dishes, but she hasn't actually made the request. It's much better to have a request out in the open so it can be discussed, rather than getting stuck in old patterns like giving each other the silent treatment. Talking about it will help you know where you stand.

Reinforce.

It's often helpful if you provide incentive for others to give you what you're asking for; for example, if your parents lend you the car, you'll fill it back up with gas and you'll even wash it this weekend. This way, they will be more likely to want to help, not necessarily because they're getting something out of it, but because they see your willingness to compromise and negotiate.

Since I've thrown a lot at you here, let's put all of these steps together with some examples.

Carter Asserts Himself with His Girlfriend

Carter's already lost some good friends in his band, and he certainly doesn't want to lose his girlfriend as well. Merrin has already made it clear that he has to change his ways or she's done, so he's trying to be more assertive rather than letting his anger control him. He wants to talk to Merrin about her threat to leave so she knows he's taking it seriously. Here's an example of how Carter might speak with Merrin:

(Describing the situation) You've told me that you're ready to end our relationship if I can't get my anger under control. **(Stating opinions and emotions)** I don't like the thought of losing you; it terrifies me, and it also hurts me to know I've hurt you so much. **(Clearly stating what he wants)** I'd like it if you could help me manage my anger by pointing out to me when you see it start to rise; I'm working on doing this myself, but it's hard.

(Reinforcing) I'd really appreciate it if you could help me with this, and it just might save our relationship.

Here you can see Carter incorporating all four steps in what he's saying to Merrin. He's not judging her or blaming her for the situation. By describing the situation, he makes sure they both know what's being discussed, and Merrin has an opportunity to correct any errors in Carter's perceptions. He's very clear about what he's asking Merrin to help him with, and the reinforcer is both his appreciation and the fact that it might help their relationship. This is assertive communication!

Rebecca Asserts Herself with Her Mom

Rebecca has been feeling neglected by her mom, who had always made her a priority until she became involved with her new boyfriend, Tom. Following is how an assertive conversation might start with Rebecca asking her mom to spend more time with her.

(Describing the situation) You've been spending a lot of time with Tom recently, which means we haven't been spending as much time together as we used to. **(Stating opinions and emotions)** I really miss spending time with you, and I've been feeling very alone. **(Clearly stating what she wants)** I'd really like it if we could spend the weekend together, just the two of us. **(Reinforcing)** I think it would help us reconnect, and it would make me feel better.

Again, you see here that Rebecca just describes the situation, matter-of-factly and without blaming her mother. Although she doesn't state an opinion, she's clear about her emotions.

She assertively asks for what she'd like: to spend the weekend together. And the reinforcers are that it's going to be good for their relationship and help Rebecca feel better. It's clear, it's straightforward, it's assertive!

Keeping in mind that Rebecca and Carter might not get what they're asking for, I hope you can see that even if that's the case, they haven't done any further damage to their relationships, and they're likely to feel good about the way they've interacted with the people they needed to communicate with, which will increase their self-respect.

Additional Skills for Assertiveness

Here are some additional skills to help you get what you want, as well as to make it more likely that you'll maintain a good connection with the other person and feel good about yourself after the conversation.

Listen, Be Interested, and Validate

It will go a long way if others feel that you're genuinely interested in what they have to say. Start by eliminating potential distractions—turn off the TV, take your earbuds out, close your laptop, put down your phone. Make good eye contact and really focus on what the other person is saying to you. Ask questions to make sure you understand and to further show your interest. Pay attention to how often you use the word "I" in a sentence, and if it's coming up a lot, see if you can reduce it—it's not all about you!

Empathy also goes a long way toward improving your relationships with other people. Empathy is about putting yourself in another's shoes and trying to understand that person's perspective. It also has the effect of increasing your own warmth and genuineness as a human being, and it helps you feel more connected to others—and them feel more connected to you—because you understand and care about them and their feelings. People tend to be drawn to others who have the quality of empathy.

Try this: Ask someone you care about how his day was today. (You can even tell him ahead of time that you're trying something new, in case asking feels strange or uncomfortable for you.) As he's telling you about his day, try to visualize or imagine in some way what he's describing to you. Practice your mindfulness here—really pay attention to what you're hearing! Once you've heard the story, see if you can imagine what you might be feeling if this experience had been your own, and ask the person whether he's feeling this way: "I'd imagine you'd be feeling quite tired after a day like that" or "Did that leave you feeling frustrated?" If you think you're lacking in the empathy department, this is something you'll really want to work on.

Be Gentle and Use Humor

Just because you're asserting yourself doesn't mean you have to go all serious! Laughter, smiling, and appropriate use of humor can lighten the mood and be very helpful with this type of communication. Even if the conversation is a serious one, as in our examples of Carter and Rebecca earlier, being gentle and using an easy manner will help defuse tension and increase the likelihood of a positive outcome for the interaction and the overall relationship.

Another issue I run into a lot is that people tend to go into situations like these already thinking of them as problems or conflicts. Remember, it's just a discussion right now! It's just you making a request (or saying no). Come back to the present moment (practice mindfulness), and don't anticipate that it will be anything but a conversation.

Know Your Values and Stick to Them

In order for you to feel good about yourself after the interaction, it's important that you stick to your morals and values, which means, first of all, knowing what these are. Remember to think about how you would like to be treated if roles were reversed. You probably wouldn't want to be yelled at or called names or blamed; if so, these are some of your values. So don't yell at the other person, call him names, or blame him.

Avoid Arguments

Hopefully, getting stuck in arguments and power struggles also goes against your morals and values. Often, there is no winning an argument; both parties are caught up in emotions and feelings of self-righteousness, and in that moment, neither is likely to give way—unless, of course, one of them is becoming more mindful and suddenly realizes the futility of the argument! If you can use assertiveness skills to help you understand the situation better, you can shut many arguments down (or not let them start in the first place), and open the door to discussion and compromise.

Still, it is just part of human nature that arguments are going to happen; there's no avoiding them altogether. The idea here is that you want to limit them as much as possible since they really don't get you anywhere other than stuck. Above all, though, you can't avoid the *problem*. Letting the problem turn into an argument will usually increase frustration on both sides, but you can certainly discuss a problem without this happening.

Stop Overapologizing

This takes us back to that good old self-esteem conversation. People who have low self-esteem often have a tendency to over-apologize, which means they apologize for things that aren't actually their fault, that are in fact often completely beyond their control. If something isn't your fault, you shouldn't be taking responsibility for it. Of course, if it *is* your fault, take responsibility and say you're sorry.

It's important to recognize, however, that if someone experiences an emotion because of the conversation you're having, you're not responsible for his emotions. All you're responsible for is your own behavior, so you need to focus on being assertive (which, remember, includes being respectful), and let the other person be responsible for his own reactions. To go back to our example with Carter, if Merrin becomes angry with him for what he said to her, that's Merrin's responsibility to deal with. Carter has nothing to apologize for, because he didn't say anything that was hurtful, blaming, or judgmental, nor could he have anticipated that Merrin might interpret what he said in that way. Bottom line: take responsibility for yourself, and let others do the same. If you experience feelings of guilt, hold on to those—we'll be dealing with them in chapter 4!

65

Here are some general questions you can ask yourself in order to help you be more assertive:

- If I were the other person, how would I want to be treated? Alternatively, how would I want the other person to treat me?

- How can I make this person want to help me? (Remember, be willing to give in order to get; try to negotiate and compromise so that others see you're concerned with their needs as well as your own.)

- If I yell (argue, call names, and so on), how am I going to feel about myself later?

- If I yell (argue, call names, and so on), how will the other person feel about me?

- If people I respect and care about were watching me right now, would I feel comfortable continuing to behave this way, or would I be embarrassed about my behavior?

Your Next Steps

Hopefully you've continued to use the mindfulness skills you've learned so far. Now, of course, you've got lots of information about how to communicate in healthier ways. First off, you need to continue increasing your awareness of what your typical communication style is; remember, you can't change something until you've become aware of it.

As you continue to observe the way you communicate with others, you'll also want to do your best to change it when it's not assertive. If you notice you're getting stuck in a power struggle with your parents or a teacher, do your best to remove yourself from the situation so you can take some time to think about how you'd like to respond, rather than just reacting emotionally.

You can also practice the following technique, as a mindfulness exercise. Progressive muscle relaxation (PMR) was developed to help us relax, and while relaxation's not the goal with mindfulness, it can certainly be helpful, especially when there's a tendency to get anxious in certain situations. (Hmmm, like in social interactions?) So to help reduce your anxiety and allow you to communicate more effectively over the next week, try this.

Exercise: Progressive Muscle Relaxation

Sitting in a comfortable position, focus on each group of muscles one by one. Beginning with your toes, tense each group of muscles, concentrating only on that feeling of tension. Hold the tension for a count of five, and then release it. How do your muscles feel in that area before you tense them? How do they feel while you're holding the tension? And how do they feel afterward?

Slowly, in this same way, work your way up through the front (shins) and back (calves) of your lower legs and then your upper legs (quadriceps and hamstrings); your buttocks and thighs; your back (you can tense your back by arching it, but don't hurt yourself); your arms and wrists (flex your biceps, make your hands into fists, and bend your fists toward your face); your stomach; your shoulders (scrunch them up to your ears) and neck (slowly rotate your head, noticing the tension shift as you move your head); and finally your face, including your jaw (hold your mouth open as wide as you can) and your brow and eyes (squeeze your eyes shut and wrinkle your nose and forehead). Take your time between muscle groups, noticing the difference in the feelings you're generating. Focus all your attention on the action of tensing and releasing these muscles. Remember you're doing this mindfully—if you notice your mind has gone to other things, don't judge yourself, but bring your attention back to the sensations.

Practicing PMR will help you learn to relax your body more, and practicing it mindfully will also help you become more familiar with the feelings in your body, which can be excellent clues to your emotions and thoughts. In the next chapter we'll begin looking at emotions: how these can get in the way of interactions and therefore have long-term consequences for your relationships, and what you can do about this.

Chapter 4

How Up-and-Down Emotions Fuel the Relationship Roller Coaster

You can't really learn how to improve your interactions with others without learning at least a bit about how to manage your emotions in healthier ways. This is because your emotions can have such a huge influence on your behavior, and of course your behavior is going to have consequences for your relationships. So in this chapter, you're going to learn some skills to help you manage your emotions. We'll look at the importance of being able to name the emotion you're feeling, with a focus on the main emotions that often get in the way in social situations; the functions your emotions serve; and the connection between your emotions, thoughts, and behaviors. In addition, you'll learn how to use mindfulness and other skills to help you handle your emotions in healthier ways.

You might believe that you already manage your emotions pretty well, and that could be true. But even if that's the case, I'd still encourage you to read through this chapter—you can never be too good at managing your emotions, and there's always the possibility you might learn something new!

Awareness of Your Emotions

Do you ever find yourself in an emotional fog? Do you notice that you tend to ignore or avoid the emotions you're experiencing, although perhaps you realize that you feel bad or upset? If that's the case, rest assured that you're not alone. Nevertheless, it's not a healthy state to be in, and if you want to manage your emotions effectively—to not let them control you and make you do things you later regret—that's something you're going to have to work on changing. The good news is, you *can* change it. It just takes work, like most everything in life!

Think about it: if you can't identify what it is you're feeling, how on earth can you figure out what to do about it in order to help reduce the emotion? And, as we'll discuss in the next chapter, it's when your emotions are intense that it feels like they are "controlling" you. You become reactive and do things you end up regretting, which can have a negative effect on you as well as on other people in your life. So, if you can figure out what emotion you're experiencing, you can decide if there's something you can do to reduce the intensity of that emotion. And reducing the intensity makes it more likely that you'll stay in control and won't do something you'll regret later.

Mindfulness of Your Emotions

You're probably not too surprised to see that mindfulness is the first way you'll be working on noticing and naming your emotions. Being mindful of an emotion means that, instead of trying to turn it off like you might usually do, you're instead tuning in to the experience and increasing your self-awareness.

Following is a mindfulness exercise to help you with this; you can do it now as you read through it, and then make sure you come back to it when you're experiencing specific emotions to help you become more familiar with them. If you've been practicing the progressive muscle relaxation from chapter 3, this exercise will come a little easier for you because you've already been tuning in to your physical experiences.

Exercise: Noticing Your Feeling

Notice where in your body you feel the feeling. What does it feel like: Is it hot or cold? How big is it? What shape does it take? Is it moving—for example, pulsing, shivering, fluttering—or does it stay still? Factually, without judgment, describe the emotion as you feel it in your body and just allow yourself to experience it.

Of course, an emotion also comes with thoughts, and you can be mindful of these as well—for example, thinking, *I'm having anxious thoughts right now*, or *I'm judging*, or *These are worry thoughts about the future*. Again, notice that this is about just describing or labeling your experience, rather than judging it in some way; for example, *These are bad thoughts* or *I shouldn't be thinking this.*

When you allow yourself to experience an emotion in this way, you're likely to notice a couple of things—first, that it's usually not quite as bad as you thought it would be! Painful emotions often become even more painful because of how you interpret them. Take the example of Caitlyn and her social anxiety. The moment she starts to feel anxious, she starts to worry: *What if someone notices and starts to tease me? I'm going to look crazy; everyone will think I'm nuts. I have to get out of here or things are going to get a whole lot worse.* As you can see, Caitlyn's thoughts about the anxiety actually increase her fear. If she could be mindful of the experience instead of *catastrophizing* about it—in other words, trying to predict the future and expecting the worst possible outcome—the anxiety might not disappear altogether, but it wouldn't get as intense as it usually does.

Something else you'll likely notice—and might be surprised by—is that the emotion changes. If you can sit with the experience, instead of trying to make the emotion go away like so many people do, you'll realize that an emotion doesn't hang around forever. Think of emotion as being like a wave: it builds in intensity, reaches a peak, and then recedes again. And like a wave, it's impossible for an emotion to stay around forever; it is impermanent and has to change because that's its nature, like everything else in life.

Naming Your Emotion

Now that you've gotten better at allowing yourself to experience your emotion, the next step is to put a name or label on the experience. I find it easiest to help people learn how to do this by first breaking emotions down into four basic categories: mad, sad, glad, and scared. An additional category includes feelings of shame and guilt, which are a bit more complicated and could fit under the category of mad, sad, or scared—or even all three at the same time. I've grouped shame and guilt together as the experience of these emotions is very similar. The main difference between the two is that we feel guilt when we are judging ourselves (and think others are judging us) for something we've done, and we tend to feel shame when we are judging ourselves (and think others are judging us) for who we are as people. Quite often we feel shame and guilt at the same time.

Once you decide what basic category your feeling fits, you can work on narrowing it down to a more specific emotion. For example, you might be able to identify that you're feeling mad, but you wouldn't exactly call your emotional experience "anger" because that seems too strong. So your next step is to look at the following emotion list to see if you can find a word that more closely describes the emotion you're feeling. This list isn't all-inclusive, so if you can think of a better word for your emotion that isn't on the list, go ahead and use it!

"Mad" Words

Aggravated	Bitter	Enraged
Aggressive	Bothered	Frustrated
Agitated	Deceived	Fuming
Angry	Disgusted	Furious
Annoyed	Displeased	Hateful
Betrayed	Dissatisfied	Hurt

Irritated	Offended	Rejected
Livid	Outraged	Resentful

"Sad" Words

Abandoned	Disturbed	Low
Anguished	Gloomy	Miserable
Defeated	Glum	Mournful
Dejected	Grieving	Regretful
Depressed	Heartbroken	Sorrowful
Despairing	Helpless	Troubled
Disheartened	Hopeless	Unhappy
Distressed	Lonely	Worthless

"Glad" Words

Amused	Euphoric	Proud
Blissful	Excited	Relaxed
Calm	Happy	Relieved
Cheerful	Honored	Satisfied
Content	Jovial	Serene
Delighted	Joyful	Thrilled
Ecstatic	Peaceful	Tranquil
Elated	Pleased	Upbeat

"Scared" Words

Afraid	Edgy	Stressed
Alarmed	Fearful	Tense
Anxious	Frightened	Terrified
Apprehensive	Jittery	Troubled
Concerned	Jumpy	Uncomfortable
Distraught	Nervous	Uneasy
Distressed	Overwhelmed	Uptight
Disturbed	Panicked	Worried

"Shame/Guilt" Words

Apologetic	Embarrassed	Rejected
Ashamed	Forlorn	Remorseful
Awkward	Humiliated	Repentant
Contrite	Incompetent	Self-conscious
Degraded	Inferior	Self-disgusted
Dirty	Mortified	Uncomfortable
Disgraced	Pitiful	Vulnerable
Dishonored	Regretful	Wretched

Now you're on your way to being able to recognize any emotion and put a name to it, which is fabulous, but it's also just the start. Remember that being able to name your emotion is essential to helping you do something about it. Let's look now at the purpose of emotions and why we need them.

The Function of Emotions

Although emotions can often be painful, and as much as we'd like to throw them out the window sometimes, they serve some very important functions, and we do need them. Take a look at these examples, and think about some of the times when you've felt strong emotions. What purpose might they have been serving?

Michael: Guilt and Shame

Think back to Michael, the school bully. Michael picks on others to help himself feel better, and while this helps somewhat, he also feels guilt and shame about his bullying behavior. In this instance, the guilt and shame serve to alert Michael to the fact that he's doing something that goes against his morals and values. In other words, these emotions are meant to tell us we're doing something that is causing us to lose self-respect and the respect of others. And ideally, these emotions cause us to change our behavior.

Caitlyn: Anxiety

If we think about anxiety in broader terms, it makes perfect sense: without anxiety—being on high alert when we're alone in the dark or when we hear a noise we don't recognize, for example—we would have died out as a species long ago. And although we probably don't need this emotion quite as much as we used to, it still serves the same purpose. Think back to Caitlyn, who was bullied when she was younger and has developed social anxiety. Caitlyn's brain has learned that people are something to be frightened of, and in order to protect her, it triggers anxiety whenever she's around groups of people who are perceived as possible threats. Not very effective for Caitlyn now, but entirely understandable—the role of anxiety is to protect us from possible threats by motivating us to either fight or flee a situation.

If you continue to think about your own emotional responses at times, you'll probably be able to see the purpose of these emotions; for example, anger often arises to motivate us to work toward change when there's something we don't like about a situation.

Sometimes people become more emotionally sensitive, reacting more often and intensely than necessary, and reacting more intensely than would typically be warranted in the situation; for example, Carter became so intensely angry that he broke the band's equipment. But even if an emotion seems to be overly intense, you can usually identify its function. Carter was obviously angry for a reason; since anger comes to motivate us to make changes, there was likely something happening that

Carter didn't like and that he wanted to change, although he didn't go about it in a very effective way.

So far you've learned how to be mindful of your emotions, which is also helping you learn to name them. And you've learned that there's no point in trying to get rid of your emotions—that you in fact need them, and they serve a purpose. So now, let's look at one of the reasons that managing emotions can be quite difficult at times—they're often just plain old confusing!

The Connection Between Emotions, Thoughts, and Behaviors

How are you feeling right now? Hopefully you didn't say to yourself, *Bored*! But if you did, "bored" is indeed an emotion; it could come under either the "mad" or "sad" category. Maybe you said, *Like this is really hard work!* or *I feel like I'm never going to get this*. If you did, it's important to be aware that these aren't emotions—they're thoughts. Think back to our four basic categories earlier in this chapter: mad, sad, glad, and scared; *these* are the emotions. So you might be mad or sad at the thought that you need a book like this one, or you might be feeling scared about the thought that you won't be able to use the skills or that they won't help.

My point here is that we often confuse emotions with *thoughts*, and even with *behaviors*. For example, people will often express the belief that feeling angry isn't acceptable because it hurts others. But that belief isn't accurate: I can feel angry without anyone else even knowing I feel angry. It's not the feeling that is hurtful to others, but how I might choose to behave because I feel angry that might be hurtful to others. To help you understand this, take a look at the following diagram that illustrates how our emotions, thoughts, and behaviors can each influence the others.

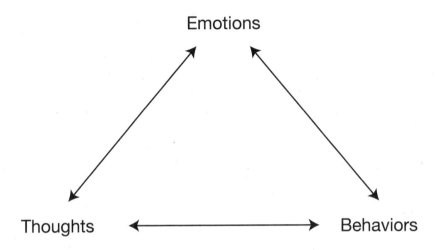

Our emotions will have an effect on our thoughts, and our thoughts will influence how we feel; our emotions will affect our behaviors, and our behaviors will also influence how we feel; and our thoughts and behaviors will both affect one another as well. Because of the connection between these three areas, we know that if we make changes in one area, the others will also be affected, and we can use this knowledge consciously to help us move in a healthier direction. (More on this shortly!)

Because emotions, thoughts, and behaviors are so intertwined, and because they often happen so quickly and automatically, it's very easy to confuse them, and especially to confuse emotions with thoughts. For example, you might think *I shouldn't have to be doing all of this extra work just to have normal relationships!* and confuse this thought with the feeling of anger. Or, you might have the thought *What if I can't do this?* and think this is anxiety. Although the thoughts here are obviously very related to these emotions, they are separate—the thought is not the emotion, and vice versa. So in order to manage your emotions more effectively, your next task is to practice differentiating between your emotions, your thoughts, and your behaviors. When someone asks you how you're feeling (or better yet, as you practice asking yourself this every day!), really think about it and work on putting a label on it, rather than just saying "fine," "okay," or even "awful." Mindfulness, of course, will also help with this. As you're noticing your feelings as described in the exercise at the beginning of this chapter, you can practice by saying to yourself, *This is the feeling of anxiety*, and *This is a thought about the future*, so that you're clearly identifying one as an emotion and the other as a thought.

Another thing to keep in mind as you practice differentiating is that a thought is just a thought, and an emotion is just an emotion; neither are facts, even though we often take them as truth. For example, just because Rebecca thinks she's unlovable, and that she has to keep giving things to and doing things for people or they won't want to be her friends anymore, doesn't mean that's actually true; it's just her thoughts and feelings about the situation. Likewise, just because Caitlyn feels anxious doesn't mean there's anything threatening her safety. This is a trap we all fall into at times: believing our thoughts and feelings to be reflections of reality. The problem is that we then end up behaving as though our thoughts and emotions are facts, and that behavior can often get us into trouble. Think about everything Rebecca does for her friends based on her emotions and feelings rather than on reality, and the trouble this gets her into. So remember: it's *just* a thought, and it's *just* an emotion. Just because they're there doesn't make them true.

Connected to this is the idea that just because you have a thought and an emotion doesn't mean you have to follow your *urge*, which is the combination of thought and emotion that often causes you to act. We've looked at the functions emotions serve, and that they're messages to take some kind of action (for example, anxiety tells you that something might be dangerous and you should get ready to fight or to run). But since you know that emotions and thoughts aren't facts, it only makes sense that you need to evaluate the urges that come along with those thoughts and feelings, rather than just acting on them. All of us have reacted from emotion at some point, and quite often it's not very helpful; when we act on an urge without really evaluating it, we often end up regretting our behavior. More on this when we get to skills!

Now that you know a bit more about emotions and their importance, as well as how we often get in our own way of acting in our best interests in the long run, let's take a look at some specific ways emotion can make social interactions difficult.

How Emotions Get in the Way of Relationships

Have you ever noticed that sometimes your emotional experience gets in the way of your ability to be effective? You might even know what you want to say or how you want to act, but the emotion you're experiencing makes it impossible for you to do what you planned. Here we'll take a look at some of the painful emotions we experience and how they sometimes hijack us and make it difficult for us to be effective in relationships.

Anxiety

Social anxiety is one of the most common mental health problems, so if you have it, you're not alone! People with social anxiety have an intense fear of being in social situations. This problem is different for everyone to an extent: Sometimes a person with social anxiety can manage social events if she knows the people she's with. Sometimes she can manage to go out with only one friend at a time without feeling a lot of anxiety. Some people with social anxiety won't have friends at all because the anxiety has completely prevented them from engaging with others. Often the person with social anxiety fears that others are judging her or won't like her, or that she'll make a fool of herself in front of others (leading to their judging her). In other words, the person with social anxiety catastrophizes, thinking about the future and imagining the worst thing that could happen in that situation. And then, of course, she assumes that that's what will happen.

A person with social anxiety tends to avoid many situations because of the anxiety, which means that her life will usually be quite limited. Is this you? Do you avoid meeting new people because you fear they won't like you or will make fun of you and judge you? Caitlyn not only avoids meeting new people but also doesn't have any friends because of her fear of being hurt by others. Even though we can understand this fear, given her history of being bullied, think of how lonely Caitlyn's life must be with no friends to share things with. (Maybe you don't have to imagine this.)

Remember, anxiety serves a purpose: it comes up to protect us. But remember, too, that sometimes people are more sensitive, and emotions like anxiety get triggered when they really have no reason to be triggered. So even though Caitlyn's anxiety makes sense given her past experiences, it no longer makes sense given what's going on in her life now.

If you are being bullied *now*, tell someone. We are much more aware of bullying and how serious it is than we used to be, and there are many services available for people who are in these kinds of situations, but you have to let someone know what's happening first and ask for help. There are also skills in this book that will help you manage the emotions around what you're experiencing, so keep practicing and keep reading.

If being bullied in the past is preventing you from moving on and developing friendships in the present, we'll be getting to more specific skills shortly that will help with your anxiety. And in the meantime, make sure you continue practicing mindfulness, since living in the present moment will reduce the anxiety and help you be more effective in all areas of your life.

Something I often tell my clients who have social anxiety is that *the world does not revolve around you*. To clarify, I mean this in a factual way, not in a judgmental way. And, to clarify even further, your world *does* revolve around you, just like the world of the person beside you on the bus revolves around her. And the person sitting next to you in the cafeteria? His world revolves around him. Get it? Most often, people aren't looking at you and the pimple on your chin. They're not thinking about your hair, your makeup, or your clothes; they're thinking about themselves, and about *their* hair, makeup, and clothes! Sometimes, putting this into perspective can be a helpful tool to reduce your self-consciousness. Do an experiment: the next time you have even an inkling that someone you trust is thinking something about you, ask what that person is thinking. Chances are it doesn't involve you at all, and if that person was thinking about you, it probably wasn't in the negative way you were assuming.

Anger

You've seen, through the example of Carter, that anger is another painful emotion that can often hijack you and get in the way of your ability to be effective in relationships. Because anger is such an energizing emotion, and the urge that accompanies it is often to lash out in some way, it can be difficult to not act on the urges that follow. Can you think of a time when you knew what might be effective for you, but you allowed your anger to control you instead? When your emotions take over and you act from your anger, you often push people away (like Carter did with Merrin and his friends). Even though acting on the emotion might feel satisfying at the time, it alienates others and often results in your being isolated and lonely.

Sometimes anger is also a kind of defense mechanism. If you keep yourself cloaked in anger, you'll be less likely to get hurt yourself. If you're always in attack mode, ready to hurt others, others will be less likely and less able to hurt you first. So if you find that anger is present in your life on a regular basis, you may need to do some work figuring out (on your own or with some professional help) what the purpose of the anger is before you can start to work on letting it go. The good news is that many of the skills in this book will help reduce your anger as well as help you learn to express it more effectively when it does arise.

Sadness

I mentioned earlier that sadness often leads to withdrawal and isolation, and this can have obvious negative consequences for your relationships. If you've experienced intense sadness—or even depression—that's led you to isolate yourself, have you noticed what this does to your relationships? Sometimes people hang in there; even when you don't return your best friend's calls or you continually cancel plans with her, she knows that this isn't you, that there's something preventing you from being her best friend right now. But many people don't see this, and that means that you may end up losing many relationships because your sadness gets in the way.

You might also have noticed that, even when you can still maintain friendships to some extent when you're feeling sad for long periods, the way the sadness influences your thinking can also push people away. People can only be around the negativity that often accompanies sadness for so long before they start choosing to limit their contact with you. Although it's not your fault—you've been hijacked by your sadness—the emotion that's bringing you down also brings the people around you down and ends up getting in the way of your relationships.

Shame and Guilt

Shame and guilt are two other emotions that tend to make you want to withdraw from others and hide away—especially shame, because it has to do with how you feel about yourself as a person. When you're only feeling guilty, you can at least rectify the problem and the guilt will dissipate; for example, you can apologize to a friend for having said hurtful things and move on, because your guilt was about your behavior. But when you're feeling ashamed, how you think about yourself as a person is affected by the behavior you engaged in. In other words, apologizing for the hurtful things you said will cause the guilt to dissipate, but when you're ashamed of yourself, the feeling of worthlessness that stems from the behavior doesn't disappear so easily.

The feeling of shame can be so intense and distressing that it convinces you that your thoughts of being worthless, unlovable, and so on are true, and when you think of yourself in these ways it limits your ability (and desire) to engage with other people. What if they find out who you really are, and what you're really like as a person? Often people won't take this risk, and they isolate themselves. Sometimes the feeling of shame can become so intense that the urge to isolate and withdraw is taken to the extreme, with thoughts of suicide. If this is ever something you experience, please talk to someone—you don't have to go through this alone, and you can get through this with help.

Acting Opposite to Your Emotion

At this point you have a basic understanding of what you need to know about emotions in order to start practicing more specific skills to help you manage them. Remember the connection between your emotions, thoughts, and behaviors? Remember how, if we make a change in one area, the others will be affected, and that we can use this knowledge consciously to help move our emotions, thoughts, or behaviors in a healthier direction? Well, here's the DBT skill that helps you do that: acting opposite to your emotion. This skill has you identify the emotion you're experiencing and the urge that's attached to it, and then act in a manner opposite to that urge. The idea is that, when you act on your urge, the intensity of the emotion you're experiencing increases. Think about it: If you're feeling angry and you yell at someone or start an argument, does your anger go down? No, it stays the same or even increases. When you're feeling anxious about doing a presentation at school and you avoid it by pretending to be sick that day, does your anxiety go down? No, it probably goes up. So if acting on your urge increases the intensity of your emotion, doesn't it make sense that doing the opposite of the urge will help the emotion go down? Let's take a look.

• Michael Acts Opposite to His Emotion

Michael's mood has been lower than usual lately, and as a result he's been spending a lot of time by himself in his room. He just doesn't feel like being around other people, and spending time with his parents kind of makes things worse since they don't really seem to understand him. Michael and his therapist have talked a lot about this, and with his therapist's help he's come to realize that isolating himself like this actually makes things worse. He knows that even though he doesn't feel like being social when he's down, once he gets out and spends time with others, he always ends up feeling better, even if only a tiny bit. So he texts his friend Kevin, and they agree to meet up to see a movie.

Michael's depression doesn't necessarily disappear, but he's providing himself with the distraction of spending time with Kevin and watching a movie, rather than staying alone in his room, where he likely would've just been thinking about how awful things are and making himself feel worse in the long run.

Like Michael, when we feel depressed we usually have an urge to isolate ourselves. When we're anxious, the urge is to avoid or escape from whatever is causing the anxiety. Quite often, we go along with these urges because it feels like the "right" thing to do, but as mentioned earlier, acting on our urges usually just intensifies the emotion we're experiencing and might bring up other emotions, too. For example, if you're feeling angry and you act on the urge to yell at the person you're angry with, you're fueling your anger and probably not acting in a way that's consistent with your morals and values, which can trigger feelings of guilt and shame. Acting on the urge to isolate yourself when you're feeling depressed usually makes you feel more alone, which feeds into your sadness. And acting on the urge to avoid situations because you're feeling anxious only increases your anxiety in the long run, and probably triggers other emotions like sadness and frustration because you can't do the things you'd like to do.

It's important to know that acting opposite to your emotion is a skill you should use only when it's not helpful for you to continue feeling that specific emotion. Remember, emotions serve a purpose, and we're not trying to stuff them or ignore them. But when an emotion has delivered its message—in other words, you know how you feel about a situation and you're ready to do something about it—the emotion itself sometimes gets in the way of your ability to act effectively. When an emotion remains intense, it can be difficult to get yourself to act in healthy, helpful ways. For example, if you're feeling anxious about going to a party, the intensity of your anxiety can get in the way of your meeting new people and having a good time. So the thing to keep in mind with this skill is that, if the emotion you're experiencing is no longer helpful and you want to reduce it, then act opposite to it. Look at the following chart to see how you might use this skill with painful emotions.

Emotion	Urge	Opposite Action
Anger	To attack (verbally or physically)	Be respectful or civil; or, if this feels too difficult, gently avoid the person.
Sadness	To hide away from others, isolate yourself	Reach out to others.
Anxiety	To avoid whatever is causing the anxiety	Approach the anxiety-provoking situation or person.
Guilt	To stop the behavior causing the guilt	If you have not acted against your morals or values, continue the behavior.
Shame	To stop the behavior causing the shame; and to hide away from others, isolate yourself	If you have not acted against your morals and values, to continue the behavior; and to reach out to others.

A last point about using this skill with anger: Anger doesn't just affect your actions; it also affects your thoughts about a situation, usually in the form of judgments. So when you're practicing this skill and trying to act opposite to your anger, you also need to think opposite, or in a nonjudgmental way. In other words, when you're feeling angry with your mom, it's not enough to gently avoid her; you also have to work on not ranting about her in your thoughts. Thoughts like *She's so mean and she never lets me do anything* will keep the anger going. We'll be looking more at this skill in chapter 6.

Your Next Steps

Of course, you're going to be practicing the skill of acting opposite to your emotion that you've just learned. And, of course, you're still going to be practicing mindfulness formally—doing your breathing exercises, practicing your progressive muscle relaxation mindfully. And informally, you'll be bringing mindfulness to activities throughout your day so that you're more aware of yourself and what's happening around you, noticing when you're living in the past or the future and bringing yourself back to the present, and practicing acceptance of whatever you happen to find in the present moment.

In addition, continue using the exercise you learned at the beginning of this chapter, which has you being mindful of your emotions. Again, even if you think you're already able to identify and name your emotions, this exercise will help you to increase your awareness, which is always a good thing!

It will also be helpful for you to practice mindfulness of the positives in your life. Every day, write down just one positive thing that happened. It doesn't have to be anything huge, like making a new friend—although imagine how great that would be! Rather, focus on the small things: Say the sun's shining today, or it's Saturday and you don't have to go to school. Maybe it's the five minutes you spent mindfully petting your dog or cat, or the movie you watched that made you smile (even if it was only briefly!). The idea here is that the more you focus on something, the bigger it gets. If your focus is all about the negative, then that's what becomes big in your life. Instead, we want you focusing on the positives so that those grow in number and become more a part of your life. And they will, with time and practice.

Chapter 5

Stop Letting Your Emotions Control You

The way we act on a daily basis is often based on mindlessness. Most people don't stop to think too much about what they say or do; rather, their words and behaviors are based on patterns or habits, as well as on the emotional state they're in at the time. Ending this "automatic pilot" behavior, however, will not only help you feel better about yourself but will also improve your relationships and reduce conflict and misunderstandings. This chapter will introduce you to some skills that will help you reduce the intensity of your reactions, thereby improving your ability to interact with others in healthy ways.

The Thinking Styles

It's important to recognize that we all have three ways of thinking about situations: from our reasoning self, from our emotional self, and from our wise self. In this section, we'll look at each of these perspectives or thinking styles, and you'll learn how to identify them—as well as how to get to the preferred way of thinking about a situation, which is by using your own inner wisdom.

The Reasoning Self

When you're in your *reasoning self*, you're using straightforward, logical thinking; either there are no emotions involved, or they're minimal and not influencing your behavior or thought process. You might be using this thinking style when, for example, you're sitting in math class trying to figure out a problem; you're doing research for an essay or studying for an exam; or you're making a list of the things you need to buy for the party your parents are letting you throw for graduation. When you're engaged in such activities, your emotions, if there are any, aren't influencing how you behave. Rather, you're focusing on the task at hand and the steps you need to take to complete it. Here's an example.

• Rebecca Uses Her Reasoning Self

After Rebecca asserted herself effectively, her mother agreed to spend the weekend with her, and asked her to make the plans. Usually Rebecca would rely on her mother to do this. But, wanting to make their weekend successful, Rebecca did some Googling to find activities in their area and made a list of possibilities. She then spoke with her aunt to get her opinion on what activity her mom might enjoy the most. Based on her aunt's opinion, the cost of the activities she was considering, and the distance they would have to travel to do the various activities, Rebecca decided she and her mom would go to the zoo for the day. Next, she went online to purchase the tickets and even planned out the bus and subway route they would need to take to get there.

The fact that Rebecca was weighing the options—comparing one activity to another based on cost and distance, and so on—means she was largely using her reasoning self when she was planning this activity. Deciding on the route and purchasing the tickets online would also involve her reasoning self, as she gathered her information and decided what type of tickets they would need; these activities would likely be done without emotion, using strictly logical thinking.

As you can see from this example, using your reasoning self isn't a negative thing. However, some people have a tendency to rely on their reasoning selves too much, not allowing their emotions to play a role in their behavior or decision making. Remember earlier in this book when we talked about balance? Acting from only one thinking style isn't balanced, and doing this too often can be problematic.

The Emotional Self

The *emotional self* is the flip side to the reasoning self. While spending too much time in your reasoning self can cause problems, the problems of acting from the emotional self are usually more noticeable because its style of thinking often tends to get you into trouble. You know you're thinking from this perspective when your behaviors are being controlled by your emotions. Typical examples of this would be when you're feeling angry at someone and you talk about him behind his back or post something hurtful about him on Facebook, or when you're feeling anxious and you avoid what's causing the anxiety.

But you might also act from your emotional self with pleasant emotions—for example, if you get a letter of acceptance from your first-choice college and call all your friends and family to share your excitement. When you act from your emotional self when overtaken by a pleasant emotion, though, it doesn't usually have the negative consequences that acting from a painful emotion does. Think back to Carter and Caitlyn for more examples of this state of mind.

Carter experiences a lot of anger and lashes out at whomever is closest—this is how he ended up alienating his friends and his girlfriend, and how the band's equipment ended up trashed. In these instances, Carter allowed his emotional self to take over, simply reacting from the anger he was experiencing without thought of what the consequences might be. Likewise, Caitlyn allows her emotional self to control her, resulting in her avoiding any kind of social situation because she feels anxious. In both these examples, Carter and Caitlyn don't allow their reasoning selves to contribute to their actions; they simply act on the urges that result from their emotions in the moment.

Just like with your reasoning self, acting from your emotional self isn't necessarily a negative thing, but when you're regularly responding from this thinking style, it will likely become problematic. So what's the solution? Again, it's aiming for balance.

The Wise Self

Thinking about things from your *wise self* is taking the balanced perspective. When you're thinking from your wise self, you're allowing both your reasoning and your emotions to influence you, and you're adding to this your inner wisdom—something everyone has. Think of a time when you had an urge to do something, but a little voice within you—whether you call it your wise self, your intuition, your gut, or something else—made you decide not to act on the urge. Instead, you realized *This isn't a good idea*, or *I'm going to regret this later*, or *I don't really want to do this*, or something similar. This is your wise self speaking.

Acting from your wise self might not be the easy thing to do, and it might not be the thing you really want to do, but somewhere inside of you, you know it's what you need to do in order to be healthy or to be the person you want to be. Let's take a look at how Michael acted from his wise self.

• Michael Uses His Wise Self

Michael ended up in detention—again. Today it was with just one other student—Pete, a boy Michael's age whom he had tormented on a number of occasions. They were to pick up garbage in the school yard for an hour after school. Michael knew that if he teased Pete it would make him feel good in the short run. It was something he often did to entertain himself, and it gave him a sense of control when so much of his life felt out of control. But Michael had also come to realize that he inevitably felt guilty later on when the pleasure wore off.

So while Michael's emotional self was urging him to be the bully to entertain himself, he knew that he would feel guilty later on. He also knew from his reasoning self that if Pete told the detention teacher or if he was overheard teasing Pete, he could get another detention, and he didn't want that. And deep down, Michael knew that it wasn't kind to treat others the way he did; there was a big part of him that wanted to stop. So in detention after school that day, Michael decided to try something different. He did his best to entertain himself in other ways instead. They weren't allowed to use their smartphones while in detention, so he couldn't listen to music, but he could sing to himself. And he practiced some mindfulness, really focusing on what he was doing and trying to be more accepting of the activity—although he didn't like picking up garbage, he tried to think of it in a more neutral way because the yard would be a cleaner, healthier place for him and the other students to hang out. While he certainly didn't enjoy his hour of detention, it wasn't miserable, and he didn't have to deal with feeling guilty or ashamed afterward.

You can see that Michael allowed himself to be influenced by his reasoning self, his emotional self, *and* his inherent wisdom or intuition—these three things put together form the wise self. You can probably also see that how Michael acted wasn't necessarily the easy thing for him to do, or even the thing he really wanted to do, but it was the thing he identified as being in his best interest in the long run.

Wise Self vs. Emotional Self

Sometimes people find it hard to tell the difference between their wise self and their emotional self, because both involve emotions; and sometimes, in the moment, the emotional self "feels" right. The key here is the phrase "in the moment." If you can delay your response for a bit—sometimes even just for a few moments—rather than reacting immediately, you'll be able to get a better feel for whether you are in your emotional or wise self. When you're acting from your emotional self, the emotions will be more intense—remember, in this state of mind, they are controlling you. When you're acting from your wise self, on the other hand, you notice and feel the feelings, but you're still able to use your logic and reasoning. You use your intuition to help you think about the consequences of your actions and decide what will be in your best interest in the long run.

Your Values Can Help You Access Your Wise Self

Michael's example also illustrates how thinking about what your values are can help you access your wise self. Michael is coming to realize that he doesn't like being a bully because he feels guilty and ashamed of himself—his behavior goes against his values of treating others more kindly and with respect. So one way of accessing your wise self is to ask yourself, *If the roles were reversed, how would I want the other person to treat me?* You can also think about someone you really admire—maybe one of your parents, a movie star like Angelina Jolie, or a human-rights activist such as Nelson Mandela—and ask yourself, *What would that person do in this situation?*

99

Considering what your values are and what kind of person you would like to be can help you make decisions based on your wisdom, rather than only on reasoning or emotions. It can help you get to equanimity, or a more balanced state of being.

What if you don't know what your values are? If this is a problem for you, consider some of these questions:

- Who do you want to be?

- How would you want others to describe you in your yearbook at the end of the school year?

- What qualities do you value in others?

- What do you admire about the people in your life you care about the most?

It can also be helpful to consider who you don't want to be. Think about someone (real or fictional) you dislike or don't have much respect for; what is it about that person that you don't like? Why wouldn't you want to be like him? Figuring out what your values are is important and will help you act from your wisdom more often, so spend some time on this idea.

How Lifestyle Choices Affect Your Thinking Style

Have you ever noticed that at certain times you just feel more emotional and have less ability to manage emotions as they come up? You can make concrete changes in your lifestyle that will reduce the extent to which you are vulnerable to being taken over by your emotional self.

Balancing Sleep

Most of us recognize that we're more irritable or grumpy if we don't get enough sleep. But have you ever noticed that the same thing can happen if you get too much sleep? You might also feel more lethargic and lack energy if you're sleeping too much. Remember, one of the keys to emotional health—and therefore to having healthy relationships—is balance, and this includes balanced sleep. When you're getting enough sleep (but not too much), you'll have more ability to manage emotions as they arise, and you'll find that you're less reactive and more able to access your wise self.

Balancing Eating

Likewise, balance is the key with eating. Ever notice how you feel if you haven't eaten enough, or if you've gone too long without eating? Most people will experience headaches, become irritable, or even notice sensations normally associated with anxiety—shakiness, rapid heartbeat, and so on. It's a fact that if you don't eat enough, you are more vulnerable to being controlled by your emotions.

On the flip side, if you eat too much you'll also be more likely to be overcome by your emotional self, especially since overeating can trigger guilt, shame, anger, and disappointment in yourself. So eating properly—having regular meals and snacks, and while not depriving yourself of your favorite foods, not over-doing it either—will make it more likely that you'll be able to access your wise self.

Getting Exercise

While we all know that exercise is good for us physically, it's also something that helps us emotionally. It's a great way of letting off steam when you have a lot of stress in your life, and it also helps you feel good about yourself because you know you're taking good care of yourself. Being physically active is also effective as a natural antidepressant and helps with overall feelings of well-being. Exercise can take many forms, and it doesn't have to be vigorous—even walking at a good pace for ten or fifteen min-utes a day is good for you. And when you're exercising regularly, you'll be more able to manage your emotions when they arise.

Taking Care of Physical and Emotional Health

We all have times when we're under the weather—a cold, strep throat, or the stomach flu. When these illnesses come up, we tend to be more irritable and grumpy, and sometimes even more needy, wanting others to take care of us. When you're ill, it's important to recognize that emotional vulnerability will be an additional challenge for you until you're feeling better. Being aware of this can help prevent you from reacting from emotions in a way that you might regret later on.

For some people, ongoing medical conditions such as diabetes, migraine headaches or other chronic pain problems, asthma, or epilepsy are also a problem. Often when these physical illnesses aren't being properly controlled or can't be treated effectively, you'll be more likely to allow your emotions to control you, and it will be more difficult to access your wise self. If you have a chronic condition, it's important that you take your medication as prescribed by your doctor and treat that illness as effectively as possible—doing this will help you feel better physically, which will have the benefit of helping you feel better emotionally.

Also, even teenagers can develop mental health problems. You read earlier about issues that can arise with depression and anxiety; bipolar disorder and attention deficit/hyperactivity disorder are other examples of mental illnesses a person might have to live with that can affect the ability to effectively handle emotions if they're not being controlled properly with medications or other treatment.

If you have a physical or mental health problem that isn't responding very well to medications—for example, you take your insulin but your sugars continue to be high, you've been taking your antidepressants but your mood remains low, or there isn't an effective treatment for the chronic pain you experience regularly—then you have to practice being aware of when the problem is worse and when it might be affecting your emotional state, again so that you don't end up doing things you regret later on. This awareness can also help you recognize when you might need to reduce your stress levels; for example, by asking for help in order to temporarily reduce the amount of responsibility you have in your life. Even though it's more difficult to access your wise self at these times, it's still possible.

So the bottom line here is, take good care of yourself when you're not well; treat your physical and emotional problems as directed by your health care professionals. And it can help to reduce your responsibilities if at all possible, as well as to practice a lot of awareness of how your illness is affecting your emotional state.

Reducing Use of Drugs and Alcohol

Drugs and alcohol alter your mood (hence the term "mood-altering drugs"!), and the problem is that you don't have any control over *how* these substances alter your mood. It's simply a fact that, when you're using, you're more vulnerable to emotions and much more likely to do things you'll later regret.

Ideally, eliminating these kinds of substances from your life would be best; then you're always the one in control, and this becomes a nonissue! But if you're not willing to do that, my suggestion is that you do your best to reduce your use, and also that you really try to become aware of how these substances affect you—not just when you're using them, but in the days after as well. I've worked with many people who, once they started paying attention, realized that not only did they have to deal with the consequences of their behavior when they were drunk or high on drugs, but they also had to deal with a hangover the next day; and many noticed that their mood remained more depressed and anxious than usual for a few days following their substance use. So pay attention, be honest with yourself about the effects of the substances on you, and then use your wisdom to decide whether ongoing use is in your best interest.

If you don't believe you can stop using substances on your own because you've become addicted or you've become accustomed to using them to help you cope with emotions, please make sure you ask someone you trust for help. Again, you don't have to go through these things alone, and in fact it's much easier if you have support. Most adults are able to set aside their judgments and help you if you can trust them enough to ask.

Using Your Wisdom to Make Decisions

As you continue to practice recognizing the three thinking styles, it will become easier to access your wise self, and to act and make decisions based on your wisdom. Remembering your values will also help. Cost-benefit analysis—thinking about the positive and negative consequences of whatever actions you're considering—is another tool that can assist you in effective decision making.

With this kind of analysis, it's important to take the time to write it down if you can, so grab a pen and a piece of paper. Think for a moment about a decision you're trying to make. For the purposes of this book, reflecting back on the section you just read, we'll use the example of a person trying to decide if he should stop drinking alcohol. If this was the decision you were struggling with, you'd lay out four boxes on your piece of paper: the costs of drinking, the benefits of drinking, the costs of *not* drinking, and the benefits of *not* drinking. Here's how you might complete this chart:

Costs of Drinking	Benefits of Drinking
• Hangover the next day	• It's fun.
• Increases my anxiety and obsessive thoughts for a few days afterward	• It's how I socialize with my friends.
• Costs money	• It reduces my anxiety (temporarily).
• Have even less control over my anger and often lose my temper, damaging relationships	
• Feel bad about myself for the way I treat the people I care about	
Costs of *Not* Drinking	**Benefits of *Not* Drinking**
• It's harder to socialize without it (more anxiety).	• I'll spend less money.
• I have to learn other ways of reducing my anxiety instead.	• I stay in better control of my emotions.
• My friends might think I'm weird if I'm not drinking.	• Less risk to my relationships
	• No hiding from my parents
	• No hangover or increase in emotions afterward
	• I have to learn other ways of coping with my emotions.
	• I might make better decisions.

As you can see, a cost-benefit analysis sometimes results in a bit of repetition; however, doing a four-box chart, rather than a traditional two-column pros and cons list, helps you see the bigger picture and identify points you might not have come up with otherwise.

Doing a cost-benefit analysis will also help you see that it's not about just comparing two columns to see which one contains more answers; rather, you're looking closely at the costs and the benefits of each behavior, and weighing the importance of each of these. Actually, if it helps, you can even take each answer in your chart and give it a numeric score so that you end up with a number value for each box. Using the previous chart as an example, the person might decide that having a hangover the next day is fairly significant in his decision making and rate it a 3 out of 5; but perhaps the lingering depression and anxiety is even more significant, and he rates that 5 out of 5, and so on. In this way, you'll come up with a numeric value for each category, which can be even more specific in helping you make your decision about whether to work on reducing a certain behavior.

When doing a cost-benefit analysis, it's extremely important that you not be ruled by your emotional self. If you are, you'll usually end up deciding in favor of whatever your emotional self is telling you to do, which is often not the wise thing. It's best to take some time and do a chart like this so that you can be sure you're thinking about it from your wise self. Doing a cost-benefit analysis can also help you access your wise self, especially when you take the time to write it down, so use this as a tool to help you when you need to access your wisdom.

Using Your Wisdom to Be More Effective

Being effective is about doing what works, or doing what's needed in the situation. It's about considering what your long-term goals are, and choosing to act in a way that is more likely to move you toward those goals. Being effective means acting from your wise self—not doing the easy thing or the thing that's necessarily what you want to do in the situation, but considering what's in your best interest and the best interests of the others involved, and doing what will be most helpful in the long run. Let's go back to our four teens and see what they could do to be more effective in their lives.

- If Carter's long-term goal is to keep his relationship with his girlfriend, being effective means learning to manage his anger so that he doesn't continue to damage that relationship. The next time he begins to feel angry, for example, even though he might want to yell at Merrin or throw his iPhone at the wall, being effective means he needs to do something different—for example, tell Merrin he's getting too angry and has to leave the situation until he calms down; or do some deep breathing or take a walk to calm himself; or lie on his bed and listen to some music he finds calming.

- If Rebecca's long-term goal is to have a better relationship with her mother, she needs to work on not taking her mother for granted any longer. So, for example, she could make a point of expressing her appreciation more often for the little things, like telling her mom how much she enjoyed the dinner she cooked or thanking her for doing her laundry. She could also make a point of trying to do more to help out around the house so that her mother sees her efforts; for example, doing her own laundry on the weekends when she's home, or offering to get dinner started on the days her mom has to work late.

- If one of Michael's long-term goals is to improve his mood, he can continue to do things that are going to help him feel better about himself, like stopping his bullying behaviors and acting in ways that are more suited to his values and the person he wants to be; for example, reaching out more to others at school and talking more to his parents in order to develop a better relationship with them.

- If one of Caitlyn's goals is to improve how she feels about herself, she needs to work on increasing her activities outside of the house so that her world can expand again, rather than continue to be controlled by her anxiety. At some point, this would also include developing some friendships, even if they're only superficial at the beginning. The point is, Caitlyn needs to practice acting from her wise self more often, rather than allowing herself to regularly be controlled by her emotions. If she can do this more often, she's going to feel good about herself, and her self-esteem will improve.

Dealing with Reality as It Is

One of the things that can often get in the way of your ability to act effectively is that you're dealing with reality not as it is, but rather as you think it should be. For example, you don't speak with your teacher about the C you got on your paper, because you think you shouldn't have to—she should have given you at least an A-. Or your best friend should have realized that you wanted to go to a certain concert because you really like the band and your birthday's coming up; but since he didn't mention it, you decide you're certainly not going to bring it up, because he should have known.

Remember, effectiveness is about meeting your goals, and this means figuring out what you need to do that will make this most likely. So if your teacher gives you a C on your paper and you think it deserves a higher mark, you need to speak with her about it, even if you think she should already know. If you want to go see your favorite band in concert for your birthday and your best friend doesn't think of it, you need to tell him you want the two of you to go to the concert for your birthday rather than not saying anything because you feel he should have thought of it on his own. Things often don't change unless you speak up; dealing with reality as it is, rather than as you think it should be, will help you move toward your goals and be more effective.

Of course, although we're talking about doing what you need to do to get your needs met, it doesn't mean without thinking about how this might affect others. If it turns out, for example, that your best friend didn't invite you to the concert for your birthday because his grandmother has been really sick and he's going out of town with his family that weekend to visit her, you have to respect his decision to put his own needs and the needs of his family before your own. Being effective isn't about being aggressive and trying to get others to bend to your will at all costs! Being effective comes from your wise self, and this means considering your emotions and your reasoning, then acting from your values.

The other important thing to remember is that while acting in effective ways will make it more likely that you at least get closer to your goals, none of these skills come with guarantees. So just because you approach your teacher about the grade you disagree with, and just because you are assertive with her, there's no guarantee she's going to change your mark. The only guarantee is that, if you *don't* make the attempt, nothing will change.

Your Next Steps

We've covered a lot in this chapter, and all these skills are going to take practice in order for you to become proficient with them. Start by paying attention to what thinking style you're using and trying to access your wise self through using the skills you've already learned, such as mindfulness and acting opposite to your emotion. You've also learned about lifestyle changes you can make to help reduce the extent to which you are vulnerable to being controlled by your emotions, and how identifying your values and doing a cost-benefit analysis can help you access your wise self. Finally, you've learned about what it means to be effective, and how you need to have goals in mind so that you can determine what you need to do in order to reach those goals.

So these are your next steps for this chapter: to continue practicing what you've already learned, to assess what lessons from this chapter are most important for you at this point in time, and to begin working on putting some of these skills into practice. Remember, these skills will help you in a variety of ways, with the end goal being that of having happier, healthier relationships in your life; as you're probably beginning to see, the skills will help you live a happier, healthier life in general.

In the next chapter, you'll learn another skill that will help you reduce your emotional reactivity, and at the same time will go a long way to help improve the way you interact with others.

Chapter 6

Reduce Your Judgments to Improve Your Attitude

Remember how, in chapter 4, you learned that how you think affects the way you feel? Well, that's really what this chapter is about, but in a very specific way: the way that your judgmental thoughts increase your anger, bitterness, resentment, and other emotional pain; and how, when this emotional pain is increased, it has more of an influence on how you behave. In this chapter, you'll learn how to change your thinking so that not only will you change how you feel, but this will be reflected in how you act toward others, which will often have a positive effect on the people around you.

What Is a Judgment and Why Is It a Problem?

First, let's clarify what we mean by the word "judgment." When we talk about judgments, we're really talking about the language we use: good/bad, right/wrong, stupid, ridiculous, and so on. Perhaps you've heard the expression "inflammatory language." Well, when we're using this type of language, we're doing just that: inflaming the situation with judgmental, blaming, emotionally provocative words. Think about how many times you judge throughout a typical day: "School sucks," "The weather is crappy," "That guy's a loser," "My parents are so mean," and on and on.

The main reason that judgments are so problematic is that, as I mentioned earlier, they increase your painful emotions. More often than not, a judgment is triggered by a feeling. Maybe you're angry at a grade you got, so "school sucks"; maybe you're disappointed you won't get to play baseball today, so "the weather is crappy"; perhaps that guy bullied you last year and so your feelings of hurt and anger cause you to call him a "loser"; and if your parents grounded you and you're feeling angry at them, you're likely to label them as "mean." So it's understandable why we judge: we're feeling hurt, angry, frustrated, jealous, and so on. But the judgment is adding fuel to the fire of your emotions. Once you start judging, your emotions increase, which causes you to judge more, which causes more emotions, and the cycle continues. And now, you're being controlled by your emotional self. Let's look at a couple of examples to make sure you get the idea.

114

- Caitlyn judges herself for her anxiety. She sees people her age getting along and managing fine, and she gets down on herself because she's different and can't do the same things other people do: *What's wrong with me? This is ridiculous; I shouldn't be anxious sitting in class. Everyone else is fine, and I can barely breathe. I'm such a loser.* You can probably see that Caitlyn's judgments are likely coming from frustration, or maybe disappointment in herself for not being able to do the things she'd like to do. But hopefully you can also imagine that Caitlyn's judgments are actually increasing her emotional pain; instead of just feeling frustrated and disappointed in herself, she's probably now feeling angry with herself, and maybe even more anxious as she wonders what's "wrong" with her.

- Michael judges his parents for not understanding him and the struggles he has with his ADHD. When his parents express disappointment in his report card, for example, he thinks: *They're totally ridiculous if they think I can do better. They're so clueless.* If Michael's parents expressed disappointment in him for not doing as well as they thought he could, it makes sense that he would feel hurt, but Michael's judgmental thoughts likely take that understandable hurt and add to it the feeling of anger.

Hopefully from these two examples you can see that judgments increase emotional pain. If it's still a little unclear, try thinking of a recent time (for most of us, there's been a recent time!) when you've vented about something. Maybe it was a grade at school or something your parents or a sibling did, or maybe it was about the school bully. Perhaps you were venting to a friend or a parent, or maybe you were just going over and over a situation in your head and, in a way, venting to yourself. People tend to think that venting is a useful activity—it helps them feel better and gets things off their chests. But we know from research that this really isn't true—in fact, venting only causes emotions about the situation to intensify; you end up reliving those emotions as though the situation were actually happening again. And what do you do when you're venting? Well, you judge, of course! So keep this in mind the next time you want to vent or rant about something—the judgments are actually just making things worse for you by intensifying the pain you're feeling. And when you're more emotional, it's difficult to not let those emotions take over and get in the way of your interactions with others.

Self-Judgments

You might have noticed from Caitlyn's example that self-judgments create just as much extra emotional pain as judging other people or situations, and here's why: when you're judging yourself, you're essentially verbally abusing yourself. If you're a self-judger, you probably say things to yourself on a fairly regular basis that you wouldn't dream of saying to others in similar circumstances. Think about how often you judge yourself: when you don't do well on a paper or exam, you're "stupid"; when you say something you later regret, there's probably a "should" (for example, "I shouldn't have said that!"); when you have a disagreement with your boyfriend, you're a "loser"; when you send a text with a typo in it, you're an "idiot."

The saying "We're our own worst critics" exists for a reason: many people are extremely hard on themselves. And when you're judging yourself so regularly, those messages stick with you and affect your self-esteem and your self-respect. You may have heard that people who are verbally and emotionally abused in a relationship come to believe what the other person is telling them; for example, that they really are unlovable and unworthy, and they'll never find someone else who wants to be with them. In the same way, you actually come to believe many of your self-judgments, and because they happen so automatically, they become a very harmful part of your self-talk. When a person's self-esteem and self-respect suffer, the likelihood of having healthy relationships lessens—think of Rebecca, who does anything she can to hold on to friends because she doesn't feel good about herself, and can't understand why others would want to be friends with her unless she does things for them. So self-judgments aren't healthy for you, and they also influence your relationships and the way you interact with others.

One quick tip here: when you notice self-judgments arise, ask yourself, *If I were speaking to my* [best friend, mother, sister, or someone else close to you], *what would I say?* Often you wouldn't say anything close to what you're thinking toward yourself, and realizing this can help you change that judgment to a more neutral statement.

Do You Push Others Away with What You Say?

Of course, judging others can be damaging to your relationships. We all know how it feels to be judged—it's hurtful, and it often causes us to feel angry toward the person judging us, and to become defensive. If you're regularly judging others, it's likely that they will choose to limit the time they spend with you in order to avoid feeling hurt and angry. Even if you're not directing your frequent judgments toward another person, people might find your negativity a turnoff and want to spend less time with you. So start thinking about what you say to the people in your life, and how this might be influencing your connections with them.

Why Do We Judge?

We all judge; it's a very human thing. And really, the question is, how could we not, given how judgmental our society is? We're exposed to judgments constantly from early in our lives, hearing that we're good or bad, that we should have done this or shouldn't have done that ("shoulds" and "shouldn'ts" are almost always judgments), and so on.

So judging becomes a matter of habit. But it's also in part a matter of convenience: judgments are short-form labels that we put on things, rather than taking the time to spell out what we really mean. For example, when you label the girl walking down the hall a "loser," what you might really mean is that you had a disagreement with her and she hurt your feelings. Or when you call your sister an "idiot," what you might really mean is that you're feeling angry with her because you're trying to get an assignment done for tomorrow and she's playing her music so loud you can't concentrate.

Before we turn to what to do about judgments, there's just one more thing you need to understand, and that's that sometimes judgments are necessary. I've come to relabel these necessary judgments as "evaluations." You need to be graded or evaluated at school in order to ensure that you're learning what you need to learn, and you need to be assessed at work to make sure you're doing your job properly; sometimes you need to evaluate whether a situation is healthy or safe for you to be in, such as when someone offers you a ride home from a party and you're not sure whether she's been drinking. You also, of course, need to evaluate whether your relationships are satisfying, healthy, and positive, or if they are unsatisfying, unhealthy, or even detrimental to you in some ways. Hopefully you can see that these are different from the judgments we've been talking about here; they're more objective and impartial.

One final point about judgments is that there are occasions when judgments don't cause extra suffering for us; for example, you might walk into the bathroom after your brother's been in there for a while and think to yourself, *Wow, does it ever smell bad in here!* While the word "bad" signals a judgment, you can probably see that this isn't a judgment that's coming from an emotion and therefore likely to trigger more emotions. In a case like this, a judgment doesn't necessarily have to be changed. But it's important to practice your self-awareness around thoughts that *are* bringing up extra emotional pain for you. If you notice your pain increase, especially with feelings like anger, frustration, or resentment, then tune into your thoughts and see if you can identify the judgments that are probably there.

How Do We Change Judgmental Thinking?

Now that you know about what judgments are and why they can be problematic, what do you do about them? Well, let's break it down into steps to make it as clear as possible, because this is not an easy thing to do!

Become aware.

You might have guessed this would be step number one: increasing your awareness of when you're judging. There will be some specific mindfulness exercises at the end of this chapter that you can practice to help increase your awareness, but for now, just work on tuning in to your thoughts when you notice your emotions increasing (again, especially the painful emotions such as anger, resentment, bitterness, frustration, irritation, annoyance, and so on). Even just becoming aware of your judgments can sometimes help you change your thinking so that you're more able to manage your emotions rather than letting them affect your behavior.

Don't judge yourself for judging!

This is worth repeating: don't judge yourself for judging. Remember, it makes sense that you judge, given the society you're growing up in. And some people grow up in more judgmental families than others—if this is you, you're probably even more judgmental than the average person and you'll have even more of a challenge with this skill. But the bottom line is, if you're judging yourself for judging, you're only increasing your judging (and heightening your emotions) ; so instead, work on just noticing it. Remind yourself it's understandable, and then go on to the next step.

Describe the facts and feelings.

This step takes a lot of practice, because it's about getting out of the habit of using those shorthand, judgmental labels, and instead thinking about or saying what you really mean. Remember, a judgment usually comes from an emotion, so first of all, see whether you can identify the emotion that's causing you to judge; as mentioned earlier, more often than not, it's feelings of hurt, or some level of anger (perhaps frustration, annoyance, or irritation). It's important to note that emotions (and this includes not liking something, being unhappy with a situation, and so on) are not judgments—they're just feelings. Expressing your emotions about something is nonjudgmental.

Once you've identified the feeling, work on describing the situation that's causing this feeling in a factual, nonjudgmental way. In other words, remove the judgmental label and replace it with the long version of what you really mean. I'm sure this is crystal clear, right? Let's go back to our earlier examples to shed some light.

Caitlyn's self-judgment was: *What's wrong with me? This is ridiculous; I shouldn't be anxious sitting in class. Everyone else is fine, and I can barely breathe. I'm such a loser.*

> **Emotion:** Caitlyn identifies that she's feeling disappointed in herself for not being able to sit in class without panicking.

> **Fact:** Caitlyn has panic attacks while in class.

> **Nonjudgmental statement:** Putting these two things together, Caitlyn's nonjudgmental statement would go something like this: *I'm disappointed in myself, and I don't like the fact that I am not able to sit through a class without having a panic attack.*

Michael's judgment about his parents was: *They're totally ridiculous if they think I can do better. They're so clueless.*

> **Emotion:** Michael identifies that he's feeling hurt and frustrated at his parents' reaction to his report card.

> **Fact:** Michael's parents are disappointed in his report card.

> **Nonjudgmental statement:** Combining his emotions with the facts of the situation, Michael's nonjudgmental statement might sound something like this: *I feel hurt and frustrated that my parents are disappointed in my report card.*

When Caitlyn and Michael can reduce their judgments in this way, Caitlyn's self-respect and self-esteem will likely improve over time, which will help her take more risks in social situations and move toward developing some friendships; and Michael will feel less angry, which might result in a reduction in his bullying behavior, and possibly improve his relationship with his parents.

When You're Trying to Be Nonjudgmental

I want to say again, this is a difficult skill to learn because judging is such an automatic behavior. Here are a couple of ways you can avoid problems people sometimes encounter when they're trying to be nonjudgmental.

Don't Rationalize or Excuse

Sometimes when they're learning to be nonjudgmental, people fall into the trap of rationalizing or excusing behavior, rather than not judging it. For example, rather than trying to be nonjudgmental toward his parents, Michael might rationalize their reaction by thinking something like, *I know they get frustrated with me and they just want the best for me.* The problem here is that, by extension, Michael is telling himself that he shouldn't be feeling hurt and angry with his parents. In other words, when you rationalize or excuse instead of being nonjudgmental, you end up judging yourself for your own feelings; as you can probably guess, and as we'll see shortly when we look at validating your emotions, this isn't helpful either.

Watch Your Tone of Voice and Body Language

Just because your words aren't judgmental doesn't mean you're not judging! You can still be judgmental with your tone of voice, your facial expression, and other body language, so it's

123

important to be aware of all of these things. Eye rolls, for example, are judgmental—you might not be saying anything out loud, but you're sending a clear message with your body language. Likewise with your tone of voice. For example, you tell your mother: "Sabrina asked if tomorrow I could drop her off at work on my way home. That makes sense." You might say this in a regular tone of voice, which would indicate to your mother that Sabrina's request is logical. Or you might say this in a tone that conveys a different message—for example, that you think Sabrina is crazy for asking for a ride. The words you use are exactly the same, but the tone of voice conveys two completely different messages.

What to Do When Others Are Judging

Unfortunately you can't control others. But hearing others judge, especially when the judgments are directed toward you, can be very difficult. Again, we've all had this experience at times, and we know how much hurt and anger it can cause. So what do you do when someone is judging you? When the school bully is calling you names? When you're fighting with your best friend and she tells you what a bad friend you are? Or when your sister tells you you're a loser?

Be Nonjudgmental

Remember, first and foremost, that if you join in the judging, you're only triggering extra emotional pain for yourself. Think of being nonjudgmental in this sense as self-protection: it has nothing to do with the other person in this situation, and everything to do with how you want to feel. So don't judge the other person for judging. Instead, describe to yourself the facts of the situation and your emotions.

Conserve Your Energy!

I remember my aha moment about judgments a few years ago. I knew it made sense to be nonjudgmental and that it was helpful, but one morning I was driving down the road on my way to work, and another driver gave me the finger (for no good reason, of course!). I became angry and started judging (and ranting and raving), and at some point I realized how much energy I was expending on this person I didn't even know. So I find it helpful to ask myself, *Do I really want to give this much energy to [this bully, this other driver, or whomever]?* This may be easier to do with people in your life you don't know well, but it can be a helpful tool to remind yourself of the energy you're spending on the other person if you continue to judge.

Be Assertive

Now's the time to pull out the assertiveness skills you learned in chapter 3 and use them! Even if the other person is judging, you can speak to her in a respectful, assertive way. This will take practice, of course, because it requires accessing your wise self—or your own inner wisdom—when emotions are more intense. But doing this will, at the very least, prevent you from making things worse; and best-case scenario, things might actually get better as you don't escalate the situation, and the other person might reduce her judgments in response. Finally, in this scenario, you'll come out feeling good about yourself for the way you behaved, regardless of the behavior of the other person.

Of course, keep in mind that the priority is to keep yourself safe. If this is a bully who uses physical violence, for example, I'm not suggesting you stick around to talk—instead, use your assertiveness skills with a teacher, a guidance counselor, or someone else who can help you in this situation. If you are a victim of violence or other abuse at the hands of anyone—parents, siblings, bullies, or others—please reach out for help; you don't have to deal with this on your own. If you don't feel you have anyone in your life you can trust with this information, there are help lines you can call for anonymous support and assistance. Abuse of any kind is not acceptable.

Positive vs. Negative Judgments

Of course, we're not always judging things in a negative way—sometimes we're actually positive! So you might be wondering, what about the positive judgments? Do they matter? The long answer is that, while it's important to be aware of the positive judgments, we're not as concerned with those as we are with the negative judgments, since it's the negative judgments that create extra emotional pain for us. However, the thing with positives is that they can turn into negatives; for example, if Michael did well on his report card and his parents told him how smart he is, does that mean if he doesn't do so well on his next report card he's no longer smart, or even that he's stupid? Likewise, if a friend you consider wonderful does something you don't like, does that make her a bad friend?

Another pitfall here is positive self-judgments: if you're used to calling yourself an idiot when you make a mistake, it's probably not realistic to turn this into a positive judgment like, *No, I'm really smart*, because you'd have a hard time believing it. So be aware of the judgments and, as often as possible, change your judgments—positive or negative—to neutral statements.

Being Nonjudgmental with Emotions: Validation

There's another important aspect to the skill of being nonjudgmental, and this is with regard to emotions; this skill is called *validation*. Essentially, validation is about accepting an experience as it is. This experience could be, for example, a feeling, thought, or belief, but here we're going to focus on validating an emotional experience. With this skill, we're not saying that we agree with the experience necessarily, but we're able to acknowledge it and understand it. It's important to validate ourselves and others, and we'll look at doing both in this section. Because we need to be able to manage our own emotions in order to have successful interactions with others, we'll start by looking at the importance of validating ourselves first.

The Messages We Receive About Emotions

We receive lots of different messages about emotions from our families, but these messages also come from our peers—including our friends—especially earlier on in our lives, and from society as a whole.

Messages from Family

There are all sorts of ways we get messages from our families about emotions. For example, you might have a family member who tends to blow up in anger. The message you might learn from this is that, in order to make yourself heard, you have to blow up at other people. Or, if you're someone who is frightened by your family member blowing up, the message you might learn is that anger is a scary emotion and you should therefore stuff it and not let others see when you're angry. Another example is through more direct messages; for example, you might recall your parents telling you that you're silly for being afraid of the dark, and you therefore learn that being afraid is silly, and you shouldn't feel this way.

Messages from Peers

In a similar way, our peers can teach us which emotions are okay to feel and which ones will be judged. For example, if we feel hurt and start to cry, we might be made fun of. The lesson here might be "It's not okay to cry," or even "I'm weak if I feel hurt about things." Being bullied is an extreme form of invalidation, in which your emotions and many other aspects of your experience are judged harshly.

Hopefully people who receive such invalidating messages also have more positive interactions with their peers at times—you might have one or more friends who validate your emotions, counteracting the invalidating messages you receive when you're being bullied. Or you might have been brave enough to reach out for help from an adult, and hopefully you received validation there. This doesn't undo the damage, of course, but it can certainly help if you're not hearing just that invalidating message all the time, but have someone else who's supporting you and telling you it makes sense and is okay that you feel the way you do.

Messages from Society

Of course, society also plays a role in teaching us certain things about emotions. For example, one well-known stereotype is that boys shouldn't cry. Some boys will take this to heart and think that they are weak if they cry, or that it means they are defective in some other way. Many people learn from stereotypes that anger is a "bad" emotion and should be suppressed; this can lead to beliefs about anger such as "I'm a bad person if I feel angry," or "It's wrong to be angry."

We all develop different beliefs about emotions based on the experiences we have with them and based on the messages we've received throughout our lives. Some people are more sensitive and will take such messages more to heart than others. Some people grow up just knowing that emotions are part of the normal human experience and are okay to feel, in spite of the messages they receive. But most of us grow up internalizing these messages at least to some extent, and this leads to our invalidating at least some of our emotional experiences.

129

Invalidating Your Emotions

When you invalidate your emotions, you're judging yourself for having that emotion. Think back to the example of Caitlyn earlier in this chapter. Caitlyn was judging herself for feeling anxious and invalidating her anxiety—telling herself she shouldn't be feeling it, and that there was something wrong with her for being anxious. And remember the emotions that came up in Caitlyn because of this? She was disappointed in herself and frustrated.

Often when you invalidate yourself, you intensify your painful emotions. You start off with a *primary emotion,* or a feeling that arises in response to a situation, and when you judge yourself for feeling that primary emotion, you increase your painful feelings by generating *secondary emotions,* or feelings about your feelings. One of the main benefits to validating yourself, therefore, is to keep other painful emotions at bay. When you're not generating those extra painful emotions, you're more able to access your inner wisdom, which can help you figure out if there's something you can do to make the situation better in some way.

Of course, keeping your emotions from becoming more intense is also going to help your interactions with others go more smoothly and will reduce the likelihood of taking your emotions out on the people around you, which is likely to have a positive impact on your relationships.

Validating Yourself

Think of this skill as being nonjudgmental with your emotions. In other words, when you notice you're judging yourself for feeling a certain way, change that judgmental thought to a neutral or nonjudgmental statement. Again, let's break this down to make it clearer, and then we'll look at a few more examples.

Notice.

Surprise!—here it is again. The first step, as always, is to become aware of when you're invalidating yourself. Just like with self-judgments, noticing when your painful emotions (especially some kind of anger toward yourself) start to increase will be a big clue for you that self-invalidation is going on.

Name the emotion.

The next step is to figure out what primary emotion you're experiencing; name the emotion, using your skills and referring to the list of emotions in chapter 4 if you need to. Often the hard part here is figuring out what emotion is the primary one, especially when you're feeling a few different feelings all at the same time. See whether you can figure out which emotion came first in response to the situation you were dealing with, and which emotions are how you feel about your feelings. This will often take practice, so have patience.

Identify the invalidating thought.

Ask yourself, *What is my judgment about this emotion?* Sometimes you'll know without having to think about it why you're judging the emotion and where the message came from that's causing you to judge your experience now. Sometimes you might not be able to figure this out right away. Either way, it's important to identify what judgment you're having emotional experience so that you can change the invalidating thought.

Accept the emotion.

Once you've identified what the primary emotion is and what the invalidating thought about this feeling is, you can work on accepting it. The good news here is that acceptance doesn't have to be anything fancy—it can be as simple as just acknowledging or naming the emotion, and putting a period on the end of the sentence instead of continuing down the road of judging the emotion. Sometimes, of course, it can be more than this—you might be able to give yourself permission to feel the emotion, or you might even be able to tell yourself, *It's understandable that I feel this way.* All of these actions are validating.

It's important to note that validating your emotion isn't going to make the feeling go away. But it will prevent you from triggering the secondary emotions that intensify your painful feelings. Now let's put this into practice with some examples.

Sitting in class, Caitlyn was feeling anxious to the point of having panic attacks. She judged herself for feeling anxious, thinking, *What's wrong with me? This is ridiculous; I shouldn't be anxious sitting in class. Everyone else is fine, and I can barely breathe. I'm such a loser.*

> **Notice:** Caitlyn notices that she's not feeling just anxious now but also disappointed and frustrated with herself. This gives her a clue that she's invalidating herself.

> **Name the emotion:** It doesn't take too much for Caitlyn to figure out that her primary emotion is anxiety, because she knows that school often triggers this feeling for her (it's the primary emotion because it's the emotion that's arisen in response to the situation—sitting in class); and she knows that this is the feeling she's invalidating.

Identify the invalidating thought: Caitlyn recognizes that the main judgment is *I shouldn't be feeling anxious.*

Accept the emotion: Caitlyn changes her judgment to the neutral thought *I feel anxious sitting in class.* Instead of invalidating her anxiety, she just acknowledges it.

Let's also go back to Michael's situation with his report card. His parents are disappointed by his report card, and he's understandably hurt by their reaction. Let's say Michael is invalidating himself for feeling hurt, thinking *This is stupid. I'm not a kid anymore;* here's how he might use validation.

Notice: Michael notices that now, in addition to feeling hurt, he's feeling angry at himself. This additional emotion gives him a clue that he's invalidating himself.

Name the emotion: Michael acknowledges his primary emotion: that he's feeling hurt by his parents' reaction. He sees that the anger he's now feeling is the secondary emotion, in response to his self-judgments about feeling hurt.

Identify the invalidating thought: Michael realizes that he's judging himself as being childish for feeling hurt, and thinking he shouldn't feel that way.

Accept the emotion: Michael changes these invalidating thoughts to just acknowledge the feeling: *I feel hurt that my parents are disappointed in my performance.*

Remember, the primary emotions Caitlyn and Michael are experiencing aren't going to miraculously go away—but when they can acknowledge their anxiety and hurt as they did in these examples, they won't be intensifying their pain by generating secondary emotions.

Validating Others

Let's take a brief look now at how you can use this skill to improve your connections with the people in your life. Now that you know how good it feels to be validated by others—to have someone tell you that your emotional reaction is understandable, it makes sense, and even that it's okay that you feel this way—it's important that you be able to do this for the people in your life as well. It helps you connect with others and helps them feel understood by you, which goes a long way in improving relationships.

When you're validating others, you want to express acceptance and understanding of their internal experience—again, whether it's an emotion, thought, belief, or something else. Here are some tips to help you get started.

- Start by paying attention and showing interest in what the other person is saying; this shows her that you care, that what she's saying is important to you. You'll have to put your mindfulness skills to use once more and bring your full attention to the interaction. Turn off the TV, put your books away, close your laptop, and listen. Notice when your attention starts to wander, and make a point of bringing your attention back to the conversation.

- Reflect back to the other person what she's saying periodically, so that you both know you're understanding her correctly. Sometimes you can guess what the other person might be thinking or feeling in the situation, or you can pick up on clues in her facial expression, tone of voice, and so on, that tell you she's probably thinking or feeling certain things. When you can point out things that the other person is leaving out of the story (for example, "It seems like you feel pretty angry about this"), she will likely feel really understood.

- It will also be helpful for you to pay attention to how much you're contributing to the conversation. Remember to notice how often you're saying "I." When you're trying to be validating, it's more about the other person than it is about you, so keep your "I's" to a minimum!

Asking questions, really paying attention, showing you're interested, and accepting the other person's experience will go a long way in improving your relationships with others.

Your Next Steps

Of course, these skills often don't come easily. Noticing when you're judging or invalidating yourself or others takes a lot of awareness, which means practice. In this final part of the chapter, I've outlined a couple of mindfulness practices that will help you become more aware of your thoughts. When you've been practicing these kinds of exercises for a while, you'll start to become more aware of your thoughts naturally, which will improve your ability to notice the judgments that might follow and then do something about them. So over the next couple of weeks, really work hard on practicing these exercises.

Begin by reading through one exercise to familiarize yourself with it; then put the book aside to actually practice it. You might find that you have a preference for one exercise over the other, which is fine, and you can certainly stick to the one you prefer. If you don't have a preference, feel free to alternate between the two.

Exercise: Observing Your Thoughts and Emotions in a River

Sitting in a comfortable position, close your eyes. In your mind, picture yourself standing in a shallow river. The water comes to just above your knees, and a gentle current pushes against your legs. As you stand in the river, notice as your thoughts and emotions slowly start to float down the river, gliding past you on the current. Don't try to hold on to them as they float by, and don't get caught up in them; just watch them as they float past you down the river. When you notice yourself getting caught up thinking about a thought or an emotion so that you're going down the river with it instead of just watching it float past, come back to just standing in the river. Bring your attention back to the exercise, and focus on just observing. As best you can, don't judge the thoughts or feelings that you notice as they go by; just become aware of their presence.

Exercise: Observing Your Thoughts and Emotions in Clouds

Imagine yourself lying in a field of grass, looking up at the fluffy white clouds. In each cloud you can see a thought or a feeling; observe each thought or feeling as it slowly floats by. Don't judge them, don't label them; just notice them as they float through your mind. Don't try to grab on to the thoughts or emotions, and don't get caught up thinking about them—just observe them. If you notice that you've gotten carried away with a particular cloud, bring yourself back to lying in the field of grass. When you notice your attention straying from the exercise, bring your attention back to observing and labeling the thoughts and emotions, without judging yourself.

Remember, this book is about making meaningful changes in your life, so no rushing! Take your time practicing these skills to make sure you understand them before you move on to the next chapter.

Chapter 7

Stop Fighting Reality and Deal with It Instead

We spend so much time and energy fighting the things in our lives that we don't like or that cause us pain. In this chapter you'll learn a skill that helps you be more accepting of things in your life—even when they're painful—so that you trigger fewer emotions for yourself. The end result of being more accepting is that you'll be a happier and emotionally healthier person, a person that other people will want to be around more often; and you'll have healthier relationships.

Reality Acceptance

When we talk about *reality acceptance*, we're talking about acknowledging reality as it is—and in fact, not judging it as good *or* bad. Think of the motto of reality acceptance as "It is what it is"—not in a "whatever" kind of way, but in a way that you really mean. What you're really saying is: *This is the way it is; this is reality, whether I like it or not.* Then, of course, you can look to see whether there's something you can do to change the situation if you *don't* like it.

Before we go any further, let's get you applying this to your own life. Take a moment to think about how accepting or non-accepting you are. When something difficult happens in your life, is your typical reaction to throw a temper tantrum? Maybe you yell, or you just think to yourself about the situation and how unfair or stupid or crazy it is, over and over again. Maybe you escape into gaming, or drugs, or alcohol to avoid thinking about the situation at all; maybe you hurt yourself on purpose, or you just turn to sleep in order to avoid the world for a while. We often see a lot of drama when people are refusing to accept something: the friend who keeps after her ex, trying to get him back; people lying to each other or going to extremes in other ways to make a situation more to their liking. There are lots of ways we can refuse to accept reality; these are just some of them. The problem is that refusing to accept something actually just increases your emotional pain—typically, you'll become more angry, bitter, resentful, or frustrated about the situation.

But maybe you're a person who is more accepting, at least some of the time. When you accept something, it doesn't mean that you like the situation or that you don't want it to be different; it just means that you're acknowledging your reality as it is, rather than fighting it (also known as judging it!).

To help you better understand this idea of acceptance, think of a time in your life when something painful happened—perhaps someone you loved died (a grandparent, a friend, a pet); maybe you didn't get something you really wanted (a part in the school play or a job at a specific store); maybe something really painful was happening in your life (like being hurt in some way by someone you trusted, your parents telling you they're splitting up, or seeing someone you really like in a relationship with someone else).

At first, most people will fight this pain—you judge it, you vent and rant about it, you might even shout about it, and you refuse to accept it. But typically, as time goes on, you start on the path of accepting whatever the situation is that's causing you pain. So think about this: with the situation you have in mind, what was the difference between when it first happened and you were fighting your reality (for example, thinking how unfair it is, that it shouldn't be happening, that it's horrible, and so on), and when you were able to be more accepting of it?

Most people notice a sense of relief, or of feeling "lighter," like a weight has been lifted. When you get to acceptance, the situation has less power over you. You tend to spend less time thinking about it, and when you do think about it, it triggers less emotional pain than it used to. And this is important to note—the pain doesn't go away when you get to acceptance, but your suffering decreases. There's a saying that pain is inevitable in life, but suffering is optional. This is because suffering is what happens when you refuse to accept the pain in your life. In other words, when you fight reality and judge what's happening, you trigger more emotional pain for yourself. When you get to acceptance, the pain doesn't go away, but the suffering dissipates.

Before we look at how to get to acceptance, let's look at some examples to help you understand the difference between fighting reality and accepting it.

Fighting Reality: Carter

Remember Carter's situation: he pushed away his friends and bandmates with his anger. When he initially lost these people in his life, Carter's anger took over and he fought this reality, thinking things like: *They're losers anyway, and I don't need them; We've been friends forever, and they should have stuck by me;* and *They deserve everything they got, and then some.* Carter was judging his friends for giving up on him, and he was refusing to accept his role in the outcome; he wasn't taking responsibility for his actions, but was blaming everyone else—in other words, he was fighting reality.

This kind of thinking will affect Carter's behavior toward others. So, for example, when he and Merrin are spending time together, his fighting reality is going to seep into their interactions. Carter will likely start thinking about losing his friends, which will lead to talking and venting to Merrin about it. Carter's anger (his suffering) is going to increase, which will probably become a problem in their relationship, especially since Merrin has already made it clear that Carter needs to work on getting his anger under control if he wants to stay with her.

Accepting Reality: Carter

As time went on and Carter's emotions lessened in intensity, he was able to see more clearly the role he played in this situation, and he was able to accept some responsibility: *I took my anger out on them in an unhealthy way, and they didn't deserve that; I need to learn to manage my anger in healthier ways or I'm going to lose more people in my life;* and *I can't go back and change what I did, but I don't want to keep doing the same things in the future.*

As you can see, Carter's mind-set has changed and he's become more accepting of his reality. He's stopped judging his friends, and he's not judging himself either—he's just acknowledging reality as it is, and then looking at how he can prevent himself from making the same unwise choices in the future.

Fighting Reality: Rebecca

Rebecca is still having a really hard time accepting the fact that her mother has a new boyfriend: *It's not fair that she puts Tom first all the time, and she's ruining our relationship; she can't see what a jerk he is, and she's stupid to stay with him; she's totally choosing him over her own daughter, but family should always come first.* Rebecca is feeling hurt that her relationship with her mother has changed, but her thoughts are increasing her suffering—she's feeling anger, resentment, and bitterness toward her mother and Tom. This increase in painful emotions (suffering) is likely to make things worse, as Rebecca takes the emotions out on her mother—becoming more argumentative, for example, and even saying some of the judgmental things she's thinking, which will only cause her mother to feel hurt and angry in return.

Accepting Reality: Rebecca

If Rebecca worked instead on accepting the fact that her mother has a new boyfriend, things would be quite different. By "accepting" I don't mean that Rebecca should like the fact that her mom has a new boyfriend (or that she should like the new boyfriend!), but that she should start acknowledging this as her new reality in order to reduce her suffering. To change fighting reality to acceptance, Rebecca's thinking would go something like this: *I don't like that my mom has a new boyfriend, but I can't change it; I feel hurt that Mom is spending more time with Tom than she is with me, and I miss her*; or *Even though I don't like Tom, I can understand that Mom would want someone new in her life.* By thinking about the situation in this way, Rebecca is reducing her suffering— her anger, resentment, and bitterness are going to come down or disappear altogether. Her hurt is likely to remain, because the bottom line is that she still misses spending time with her mother. But if Rebecca can reduce her suffering by becoming more accepting of reality, she'll be more able to access her wise self and therefore to have more successful interactions with her mom when she tries to talk to her about these things.

Now that you have an idea of how being more accepting of reality will be helpful for you—in terms of reducing your own emotional intensity, and also therefore in improving your ability to relate to other people—let's take a look at how you can practice this skill.

How to Accept Reality

You've probably heard that old cliché "Time heals all wounds." Well, I don't believe this is true exactly. But I do agree that, usually, the further away you move from something in time, the less painful it becomes. In other words, emotions do tend to dissipate naturally over time. At first when you lose someone, for example—whether because the relationship came to an end or because that person died—the pain might feel excruciating. But in most instances, as time goes on the pain becomes more bearable; as you get used to the loss you've suffered, your emotions gradually become less intense. Of course, the more painful something is, the longer this takes, and the same holds true for practicing the skill of acceptance: the more painful a situation is, the longer it will take for you to accept it.

The good news is, once you've learned about reality acceptance, you can consciously practice this skill to help reduce the suffering in your life; you no longer have to just sit back and wait for time to take its course.

Make the commitment.

The first step is to decide for yourself whether you're going to work on this skill. Acceptance is hard work, but I really hope you believe me when I tell you it's worth the effort in the long run. And if you don't believe me, think back to that situation in your life that started out as really painful, but didn't hurt nearly as much once you came to accept it—*that's* how helpful this skill is. If you have a situation that you're fighting (and most of us have at least a few, if not many), ask yourself this question: do you really want to continue to spend this much time and energy on this situation? If the answer is no, then make the commitment to yourself: *As of right now, I'm going to work on accepting* (name your situation here).

Notice the fighting.

The next step in accepting reality is (surprise, surprise!) to be mindful. Pay attention to your thoughts and your emotions, and notice when you're fighting reality instead of accepting. And of course, don't judge yourself when you notice that you are fighting—just accept that you're not accepting. Remember, judgments will only increase your emotions and make it more difficult for you to access your wisdom.

Talk back to your thoughts.

Once you've noticed that you're fighting reality, the next step is to turn your mind back to acceptance. In other words, you notice you're fighting reality, and you talk back to those thoughts. This turns into what I call the "internal argument." Let's take a peek at Rebecca's thoughts for an example of what this might look like.

Fighting reality: *I can't believe she's staying with that loser; doesn't she see that she's totally ruining our relationship because of him?*

Accepting: *Wait; I said I was going to work on accepting this situation, and I'm getting myself worked up again. I don't want to do this.*

Fighting reality: *But she's blind; he's so using her, and she's just throwing everything away for him.*

Accepting: *No. I'm working on accepting. Mom has every right to make her own choices. This isn't helping.*

Fighting reality: *But I shouldn't have to accept this situation; she should know better!*

Accepting: *I know that in the long run, accepting will help me feel better. It is what it is, and even though I don't like it, I can't change it.*

Talking back to those thoughts to get to acceptance isn't easy, and it takes a lot of energy, especially when you first start to practice this skill. But keep reminding yourself of those situations in your life that you came to accept; knowing how much better it feels when you get there can help keep you motivated to practice.

I already mentioned that the more painful a situation is, the harder it will be and the longer it will take to get to acceptance. But keep this in mind: If, when you start practicing reality acceptance, you find you're able to accept reality for only three seconds out of the day, that's three seconds of less suffering you've just experienced. And soon that will grow to thirty seconds, then three minutes, then thirty minutes, and so on.

Of course, once you get there doesn't mean you necessarily stay there. Unfortunately, there will be times when you might have accepted a situation you dislike, but then your dislike gets retriggered. For example, let's say Rebecca finally gets to acceptance of her mother's new relationship. Months go by, and the relationship isn't a problem for her anymore, but then summer comes. Summer is when Rebecca and her mother would usually spend a week together camping once school gets out. But this summer, it won't be just Rebecca and her mother; it will be Rebecca, her mom, and Tom. This might be enough to trigger Rebecca to not accept the situation again; she might find herself back in the "it's not fair" stage, fighting reality and experiencing a lot of suffering again. It's important to know that this is normal, and it's part of the process; you're not starting back at square one when it happens. You've gotten to acceptance once, and it will be a bit easier this time, but you do have to go back to the steps of accepting reality and put some extra energy into practicing this again.

These additional DBT techniques may help you get to acceptance:

- Taking an open posture

  When you're fighting something, you tend to take a closed stance—fists clenched, arms crossed. Taking an open posture can help you get to acceptance: uncross your arms, unclench your fists. Try to relax your muscles (do some progressive muscle relaxation if you need to and if you can). Open yourself back up.

- Breathing

  Breathing can further help you open up. Take some deep breaths; focus on your breathing. It can also help if you do a mindfulness practice such as counting your breaths (focusing on your breath mindfully, and counting each inhalation and exhalation from one to ten, over and over), in order to distract yourself momentarily from thoughts that fight reality.

- The half smile

  Turn the corners of your mouth up slightly so that you're almost, but not quite, smiling. Think Mona Lisa—a very slight smile. You might be thinking this sounds totally weird, but it really can help. There's a saying that goes something like this: "Sometimes your joy is the source of your smile, but sometimes your smile is the source of your joy." It's a basic biological fact that the expression on your face can actually influence how you feel. I'm not saying "grin and bear it," or "fake it till you make it"—this isn't about pretending to be happy. Rather, it's that by putting on a slight smile, you send messages to your brain that increase your sense of well-being. Try it; you might be surprised.

Applying Reality Acceptance to Your Relationships

Accepting reality will reduce your suffering, which in turn will make it easier for you to access your wise self and make healthier choices. Obviously this will be of benefit to your friendships and your interactions with others. Let's take a look at specific ways that accepting reality can be of benefit in your interactions with others.

149

Accepting When You've Made a Mistake

Unfortunately, making mistakes is part of being human. We all make mistakes sometimes. Sometimes we lie, or we say hurtful things to the people we care about, or we do things that cause others to lose respect for us. It's just part of life, but owning up to it and admitting you've made a mistake can be really difficult. Often the tendency is to deny it and dig the hole even deeper, or to make excuses for yourself. But making excuses usually makes things worse, often triggering anger in the people who care about you and causing the situation to drag on.

The best thing to do when you've made a mistake is to accept it—and admit it to whomever needs to hear it—and then move on. So practice acceptance: *I made a mistake. I regret what I did, but I can't go back and change it. Instead, I'll apologize (or make repairs in another way) and move on.*

The other important part here, of course, is that you learn from your mistakes and don't continue to engage in the same behaviors. People might accept your apology once, but if you apologize and then keep engaging in the hurtful behavior, they'll stop cutting you slack, and you'll find your relationships ending. It's also important that you don't continue to beat yourself up for the mistake you've made (think back to self-judgments!)— accept it, repair it, and then move on from it.

What if your apology isn't accepted? Well, you can't make someone accept an apology; you need to focus on doing what you can do as effectively as possible, and hoping for the best. If you said something hurtful to someone, apologize in a genuine way and don't say that hurtful thing again. Hopefully that person will see that you really mean it, he'll realize everyone screws up sometimes, and he'll give you a second chance. If he doesn't, you need to accept his decision and move on. The good thing is that, as long as it's clear you've learned from your mistake and are sincere in your remorse, people often will give you another chance.

Of course, having an apology rejected is never pleasant. You'll feel some emotional pain—perhaps guilt and shame, anxiety over losing the relationship, and anger and disappointment in yourself. But at least you'll know you've done your best by taking responsibility and trying to fix things, rather than compounding the problem by making excuses, blaming others, becoming defensive, or running away.

It can also help in these situations if you think about this question: If the person that you hurt were writing in your yearbook, what do you think he would say? And what would you *want* him to say? Would it be "He was cruel and didn't care too much about others," or would it be "He sometimes made mistakes but he took responsibility for them and tried to be a better person"?

Accepting the Choices of Others

It's usually harder to accept those situations over which you have little or no control, but the bottom line is that you can't control other people. You have every right to express an opinion—and the other person has every right to disregard it! At the end of the day, everyone is his own person and will make the decisions he thinks are in his own best interest. When you don't like those decisions, you need to work on accepting them anyway; otherwise, you will experience a lot of emotional suffering as you continue to fight reality.

Your refusal to accept the decisions of another person will, of course, also lead to problems in your relationship with that person. When you're fighting reality, remember that you're judging—and we all know how it feels to be judged. If you judge that person often enough, you'll push him right out of your life. Reverse roles for a moment when you find yourself in such a situation: how would you feel if this person were judging you? Probably not very good, right? Most people don't like others in their lives trying to tell them what to do; usually people like to make their own decisions. So remember: express your opinion, and practice acceptance if your opinion isn't acted on. It doesn't mean the other person doesn't value your opinion—it just means that he's making his own decision, from his own perspective.

Your Next Steps

In this chapter you've learned yet another new skill—reality acceptance. Hopefully it makes sense to you how practicing this skill will help reduce the amount of emotional pain in your life; and that, by reducing your suffering, you'll be able to be more effective in all areas of your life, including your relationships.

Remember, the less emotional pain you have to contend with on a daily basis, the easier things become. When you're regularly experiencing a lot of emotional pain, it's much more difficult to access your wisdom and to make wise choices; instead, you end up acting from your emotional self a lot, which can lead to actions you regret later on.

So your practice for the coming days is reality acceptance. Start by thinking about the situations in your life that you need to use this skill with: What aren't you accepting? What situations in your life do you fight? What continues to have a lot of power over you, so that you think about the situation frequently and experience a lot of emotional suffering every time you do? Once you've identified some situations, see if you can identify one that is perhaps a bit less painful than the others; it can be a little easier if you start practicing reality acceptance with a situation that isn't incredibly painful. This will give you some experience with the skill, as well as proof that you can do it and that it does help. Once you become more accepting of this first situation, you can move on to others; but be patient with yourself—remember, reality acceptance is a really hard skill! Also remember, if you put in the work and energy, it will get a little easier as you go.

Chapter 8

Don't Let Your Urges Control You

In the last couple of chapters we've been focusing on skills to help you manage your emotions more effectively; this, of course, will have positive outcomes for your relationships, as the intensity of your emotions decreases and you have more control over how you're behaving. But let's take a closer look now at things you can do to reduce the likelihood that you'll end up acting on urges in ways that have negative consequences later on.

Why Not Act on Our Urges?

As you read in chapter 4, an urge is the combination of thoughts and emotions that causes us to act. It could involve something as harmless as being bothered by an itch and feeling the need to scratch it, or noticing you're feeling uncomfortable the way you're sitting and shifting yourself into a position that feels better. But urges often involve things with more serious consequences, like feeling angry and having an urge to yell at your best friend or your sister, or feeling really sad and having thoughts of hurting yourself.

We all have urges at times. And we all act on those urges at times, even when doing so might have negative consequences. But this is the key—that often, acting on an urge has negative consequences. So the goal is to become more aware of when an urge is arising, which allows you to choose how you'd like to act, rather than just reacting—in other words, to access your own wisdom (your wise self) and choose whether you'd like to act on the urge or not.

Think for a moment about some of the urges you might experience that tend to have negative consequences: avoiding things when you're anxious (like social situations!) by sleeping, gaming, or using substances; lashing out at others when you're angry; isolating yourself when you're feeling sad or lonely. You might have urges to overeat or binge, or not eat at all; you might feel like hurting or even killing yourself at times; or maybe you experience urges to hurt others, physically or emotionally, when you become really angry.

Now consider some of the negative consequences of going along with these behaviors when you follow through on the urges you're experiencing. Maybe no one knows when you've acted on an urge, so it doesn't affect anyone else, but it may have poor outcomes for your health (for example, when you're eating poorly or hurting yourself) or for the way you feel about yourself (for example, you know you're avoiding something, and you feel guilty about it).

156

But often others do know: they see you hiding in your room avoiding life, or coming home drunk or high; or they're the target of your anger, and so on. When you're acting on urges in these ways, of course, your relationships will be negatively affected as well. The people who care about you can watch you do harm to yourself (or them or others) for only so long. Sooner or later, they start to burn out and have a harder time being there to support you in ways they'd like to (and in ways that you'd like them to).

One last point: you might remember from chapter 4's discussion about acting opposite to an emotion that acting on your urge actually feeds into the emotion you're having. And this is one more reason to try to access your wise self and do something different instead. But what to do?

Of course, you probably don't always act on your urges; so take a moment right now to consider the times when you've been able to act in ways that don't have those negative consequences—what did you do then? Surely there are times when, instead of yelling at your sister, you left the room, or rather than stealing some alcohol from your parents' liquor cabinet, you talked things out with a friend. Those are the kinds of things that we would consider skillful behavior; and our goal here is to get you doing more of that.

Crisis Survival Skills

Skills that help you not act on urges are called *crisis survival skills*, because they help you survive a crisis without making things worse. Since some of these skills can actually lead to avoidance themselves, it's important to first of all figure out when it's a good time to use them. So let's define the term "crisis." Essentially, a *crisis* is a period of time in which there is a problem that you're unable to resolve, and it's causing you to experience an increase in emotional distress. Because the problem can't be solved immediately, your emotional pain isn't going to go away anytime soon. These are the times when we often experience urges to do things to help us cope, and often those things have negative outcomes. So what do you do? You practice your crisis survival skills.

Be sure to remember, though, that you can sometimes overuse these skills. When you're distracting all the time, for example, you're no longer distracting, you're avoiding. And if you're overusing these skills, you might find that you're not taking care of your responsibilities—for example, your homework isn't getting done because you're playing video games all the time—or that the activity you're engaging in is actually having negative consequences rather than being neutral: for example, you're eating your favorite foods too often and this is leading to an unhealthy lifestyle. So the key with these skills is that you're using them in moderation, to help you deal with crises when they arise—remember, you want balance in your life!

Distraction

The first way of helping yourself get through a crisis is by doing things that take your mind away from a problem that can't immediately be fixed. There are lots of ways to do this, and they'll be different for everyone—what's distracting for one person may not be for the next. Take a look at the following list of activities (it's not exhaustive!) then make your own list of things that might help your mind off a problem when you're having urges that might make the situation worse.

Do a word search.

Talk to a friend.

Draw, paint, or doodle.

Go for a walk.

Ride your bike.

Look at photographs.

Eat your favorite food.

Go rollerblading or skateboarding.

Play solitaire.

Finish something you started.

Go fishing.

Clean or reorganize your room.

Meet a friend for coffee.

Think of times when you felt happy.

Give yourself a facial.

Teach your dog or cat a new trick.

Shovel snow.

Sing.

Go to a religious service.

Play cards with someone.

Look at old yearbooks.

Buy yourself something nice.

Imagine your life after graduation.

Go to a movie.

Lie in the sun.

Go somewhere you can watch nature.

Burn some incense.

Tell someone you love them.

List the things you like about yourself.

Go bowling.

Get dressed up and go out.

Read the newspaper cartoons.

Look at the stars.

Upload some favorite photos on Facebook.

Go to a pet store and play with the animals.

Take a hot bath.

Play with your pet.

Watch television.

Play video games.

Play a board game with your sibling or a friend.

Bake some cookies.

Find a fun new ring tone for your cell phone.

Listen to a relaxation CD.

Surf the Internet.

Do a craft.

Cook your family dinner.

Write a short story or poem.

Daydream.

Watch your favorite TV show.

Buy someone a gift.

Take photographs of things you like.

Go to websites to read funny jokes.

Plan your summer vacation.

Laugh.

Pray.

Go somewhere to people watch.

Smile at someone.

Reach out to someone you miss.

Plan a fun day out on the weekend.

Read a comic book.

Make something out of play dough or clay.

Update your Facebook status.

Check your e-mail.

Do homework.

Listen to music.

Go to the beach.

Polish your toenails or fingernails.

Cut the grass.

Go for a picnic.

Go to the zoo or a museum.

Invite a friend over.

Download some new music, videos, books, or games.

Experiment with different hairstyles.

Send someone a card for no reason.

Give someone a compliment.

Walk barefoot in the grass or sand.

Close your eyes and imagine yourself in your favorite place.

Play a musical instrument.

Dance.

Write someone a letter or e-mail.

Help someone.

Learn to do something new.

Visit a friend.

Go skiing or snowboarding.

Watch a movie.

Scrapbook or journal.

Play a sport you enjoy.

Do something nice for your family or a friend.

Light some candles.

Do something to please your parents.

Explore a new area in your neighborhood.

Take a nap.

Play Wii.

Go to the mall.

Go somewhere you'll be around other people, like a park.

Go for a jog.

Do a crossword puzzle.

Go swimming.

Fly a kite.

Watch funny videos on YouTube.

Ideally, you want your own list to be as long as possible—although you might not be able to make it as long as the one you've seen here! We all know how difficult it is to think straight when you're stuck in your emotional self. By making yourself a list of activities in advance, you're taking the thinking out of the equation. You don't have to wonder what might be helpful for you in that moment; you just pull out your list of distracting activities and get started. So with this sample list, the first thing you would do is a word search; but if you do that for a few minutes and you find you can't concentrate because your mind is constantly wandering back to the crisis, then you move on to the next thing...and the next...and the next. If you make it all the way to the bottom of your list and you're still in a crisis and you're still having urges, then start over at the top of your list.

I'd like to reiterate something here that many of my clients struggle with: Distraction is *not* going to make the problem go away. It might not even make you feel better, since the problem

164

is still there. The idea is that these skills help you *not make things worse*. If you survive the crisis without acting on your urges, then the skills are working!

Self-Soothing

Think about the things you find soothing, and add them to your list; some of the activities that soothe you may overlap with your distracting activities, and that's fine. Think about your senses as well: what do you find soothing to listen to, for instance? You might add to your list (if it wasn't already there) "listening to music," or "listening to nature." What about things that are soothing to see? You might add to your list, "watching my dogs play," or "looking at photographs of [someone you care about]." Then think about things that are soothing to taste, touch, and smell, and add these to your list as well.

Again, you can see how these activites aren't going to solve your problem, but they can help you get through the crisis period without acting on urges that might make things worse for you, so be sure to put a lot of thought into them.

Reframing

This is a skill that focuses more on your thinking about the crisis; again, it won't change the problem, but changing the way you're thinking about it can help you not act on any urges that might be coming up for you, urges that could result in making the crisis worse in the long run. Following are some ways you can work on reframing.

Encourage Yourself

When we think about a problem, we often catastrophize: we think about the worst-case scenario, and how awful everything is likely to turn out. Our minds also tend to take us to times in the past when we've had negative experiences, almost as though to prove to us that it can't possibly go well this time either. For example, if the crisis is that you've had an argument with your friend Gina and she isn't speaking to you right now, your thoughts might go something like this: *Great, I've screwed up another friendship. I always do this. Gina is probably never going to speak to me again. I won't have any friends for the rest of my life.* Although it's not uncommon to think like this, you can probably see that it's completely unhelpful!

So one way of reframing is to counter this kind of thinking. When you notice you're catastrophizing, try to do something different. Mindfulness, of course, will be helpful, so come back to the present and focus on the here and now. But in the here and now your problem still exists, so try to encourage yourself instead of naysaying. Try thinking things like, *It's difficult, but I will get through this* or *I don't know yet that the friendship is over.* Notice that we're not aiming for positive here—*It'll be okay! She'll come around* likely isn't going to be believable when you're in those really difficult moments, so stick to neutral instead.

It can also help if you ask yourself, *Will this matter a year from now?* Sometimes, of course, it will. But you might be surprised at how often you'll be able to see that, although the situation is painful right now, it's not something that's going to still matter in a year. Of course, this isn't about minimizing your pain. Remember the skill of accepting your emotions, from chapter

6? You still need to validate the fact that while it's not the end of the world, it's something you're really struggling with.

Compare

Another way of reframing is by comparing yourself to someone who isn't doing as well—for example: *Even though I'm stuck in this crisis, I'm not using drugs like my friend Alexandra is.* When you use this skill, it's important to recognize that it has nothing to do with putting Alexandra down—rather, it's about helping you see the bigger picture. It's about acknowledging that, although things are difficult, they could also be worse.

Sometimes, though, people get stuck on this skill. If that's you, don't throw the skill out yet. There are other ways you can do it: How about comparing yourself now to a time in your life when you weren't coping as well? For example, *Even though I'm stuck in this crisis, I'm not using drugs like I was last year when things got really hard.* Or, instead of narrowing your focus to yourself, try broadening it to a more global level. As I'm writing this book, there are countries whose citizens live in daily danger. So how about this: *Yes, things are sucking in my life right now, but at least I'm not living under the threat of war.* Hopefully you can see that this has nothing to do with putting yourself or others down, or minimizing anyone's pain, but with helping you see things from a different perspective and drop the drama. Even if it feels like it right now, is it really the end of the world?

Find Meaning

One last way of reframing that we'll look at here is through finding meaning in your experience. This is basically about not letting your suffering go to waste—is there a way that you can make your pain mean something? Let's look at Michael as an example. Perhaps, as he begins to act more and more from his own values and continues to give up his bullying behaviors, he can begin to see where these behaviors came from. Remember, Michael began to bully because he didn't feel good about himself, and because his ADHD and depression got in the way of having healthy relationships with others. So maybe as Michael grows and learns ways of managing his emotions more effectively, he can find meaning in his experience by helping others who are bullies to see that there are other ways of dealing with their emotions besides taking them out on people around them.

Your Next Steps

In this chapter we've focused on skills that will help you get through a crisis situation without making things worse by acting on urges to do things that result in negative consequences. Your main task now is to sit down and start working on your list of crisis survival skills: What can you do when a crisis strikes that will help you not act on the urges that will make things worse? What will distract you from the crisis? What will you do that soothes you? Remember, make the list as long as you can.

Something else to consider is whether there are themes in the crises in your life. Are you regularly in conflict with others? Are there things you tend to fight about with your best friend or your boyfriend or your parents? If so, you may be able to plan in advance for some of these conflicts so that you act in more effective ways. For example, if you know you regularly catastrophize about a specific situation, you could write out some self-encouraging or comparison statements now, so that when a crisis strikes you don't have to think about them; you can pull out your list and read them to yourself.

Even if you don't have themes like this, you could probably still do some preplanning: jot down some guiding thoughts on sticky notes and put them around your room so you see messages like, "Is it the end of the world?" or "Will this matter in a month, or a year?"

And remember, keep practicing your other skills as well. When all is said and done, you need to keep working on all your skills to make the permanent changes that will keep you moving toward a more satisfying life.

Chapter 9

Improving Your Relationship with Yourself

We touched very slightly on the idea of self-esteem in chapter 2, but you might think it's strange that, in a book about connecting with others, I've left self-esteem skills until last. But the fact is, all of the skills we've looked at so far will contribute to improving your self-esteem and the way you feel about yourself. So in this final chapter, we'll look at some additional things you can do to increase your self-esteem, and how this will have a positive effect on the way you interact and connect with the people in your life.

What Is Self-Esteem?

Self-esteem is essentially how you feel about yourself; if you have good self-esteem, you believe yourself to be an inherently good person. You are able to acknowledge that sometimes you make mistakes or do things you end up regretting, but even when that happens, you understand that it doesn't reflect badly on who you are as a person. It simply means you've made a mistake or done something you regret. In other words, you're human!

When someone has low self-esteem, on the other hand, he has a harder time seeing the good in himself. If you have poor self-esteem, making a mistake means that you are "stupid" or "worthless"; doing something that you regret later on means you're "evil" or "unworthy." In other words, having poor self-esteem leads to difficulties in separating *who you are* from *what you do.*

Self-esteem is different from self-confidence, and I find that people often confuse the two. You can have good self-esteem and not be self-confident, or you can have low self-esteem and still feel confident in certain situations. *Self-confidence* is more about your belief in your abilities than how you see yourself as a person. Rebecca, for example, doesn't feel very good about herself as a person and believes that people will remain friends with her only if she does things for them—this is low self-esteem. However, let's say Rebecca is really good at math, and so she's really confident that she's going to ace her math exam next week—this is self-confidence. On the flip side, Rebecca's self-esteem will hopefully increase over time, especially as her relationships improve; she'll come to see that she has value as a person in and of herself, and not just for what she can do for people; she'll come to love who she is and see that others love her as well. But even if Rebecca develops better self-esteem, there will still be times when she won't have confidence in herself; for example, when she starts learning how to play volleyball, she might not be at all confident in her abilities.

To develop your self-esteem, it's important to separate what you do from who you are. You can't control whether you get on the cheerleading squad or the baseball team; what you can control is how hard you try, and your attitude (that is, how you talk to yourself and to others) about the outcome. It's not effective to rely on external events to make you feel good about yourself or happy with who you are. We'll look at this further in a moment when we discuss core values and their impact on self-esteem.

Your Journey So Far

Now that you know what self-esteem is, let's take a look at the skills you've learned so far that will help improve how you feel about yourself.

Assertive Communication

Although it's easier to be assertive when you already feel good about yourself and as though you deserve to tell others what you want and how you feel, communicating assertively will in fact improve how you feel about yourself. It's kind of that "fake it till you make it" idea—the more you act as though you respect yourself and deserve respect from others, the more you actually will come to respect yourself and believe you deserve the respect of others!

Managing Emotions

Similarly, when you're managing your emotions more effectively—for example, doing things like acting opposite to your urge in order to reduce the intensity of your emotions, or acting from your own inner wisdom rather than allowing your emotions to control you as you used to—you'll begin to see that you can make wiser choices, and you'll start to believe in and respect yourself more.

Reducing Judgments and Increasing Self-Validation

This is a biggie: remember our discussion from chapter 6 about verbally abusing yourself when you're self-judging? Well, if you've been practicing being nonjudgmental, you've probably found that you feel better about yourself, not just for not judging others but also because you're being more gentle with yourself. Likewise, if you're giving yourself permission to feel emotions that you would previously have judged yourself for, your self-esteem will be on the rise—but keep in mind, these are tough skills to practice, so even if you haven't noticed a difference yet, keep at it!

Accepting Reality

Similarly, the more accepting you are of your reality, the less judgmental you'll be; and the less judgmental you are, the more you'll find that your self-esteem increases. Remember that fighting reality triggers a lot of anger and other emotional pain, and when you're feeling these painful emotions on a regular basis, they're bound to have negative consequences with regard to how you feel about yourself.

Not Acting on Urges

If you've stopped or at least reduced some of the unhealthy behaviors you were engaging in previously, this is of course going to make you feel better about yourself. Feeling as if you're more in control and able to make healthier choices will improve your sense of self-respect.

Mindfulness

You might be surprised that I've left mindfulness for last this time! But mindfulness, of course, is the overarching theme in everything I've just said: it's being self-aware and using your inner wisdom to make healthier choices; it's being accepting and nonjudgmental, and stopping the fighting; it's acting effectively and being able to manage yourself rather than letting your emotions make the choices for you.

Improving Your Relationships Through All These Skills

And, of course, here's the bottom line: When you're using these skills, the people in your life are going to notice. They're going to see that you're making positive changes and, as a result, your interactions and connections with others will likely improve. When those interactions and connections improve, you'll feel better about yourself, which will make you more able and willing to practice skills, which will help you feel better about yourself ... and you can probably see the healthy, exciting direction this continues to go in!

And the good news is, there's even more you can do to help yourself continue to move in this direction.

More Ways of Building Self-Esteem

Now that we've reviewed what you've already learned (and have hopefully started applying to your life) to help improve how you feel about yourself, it's not a bad idea to stop for a moment to take stock: How *do* you feel about yourself? Do you love yourself? Do you like yourself? Do you dislike or even hate yourself? Have you started using any of the skills I just mentioned to help improve the way you feel about yourself? Are there other things you've been doing to work on this? If you've been consciously working to improve how you feel about yourself, how's that going? Have you noticed any difference yet? When you're thinking about these last two questions, it's important to keep in mind that improved self-esteem, like so many other changes we try to make in our lives, doesn't happen overnight. If you've noticed small (or even tiny!) changes, give yourself credit, keep doing what you've been doing, and look to see what else you can be doing that might be helpful.

Knowing Your Values

As I mentioned earlier, you can't rely on external events to help you feel good about yourself, because you often don't have control over those events. It's not so much about whether you make the baseball team, but about trying your hardest and having a good attitude, even if the outcome isn't exactly your ideal. What these things boil down to is your core values, which we also looked at briefly in chapter 5.

Acting in accordance with your values is what will make you feel good about yourself. So whether you get on the baseball team or not, if you gave it your all, and if it's a value for you to try your best, you will feel good about yourself. You'll probably still be disappointed if you didn't make the team, but when you have good self-esteem, you won't let that external event dictate how you feel about yourself as a person. And in the meantime, the skill to work on here to develop your self-esteem is being nonjudgmental toward yourself.

When you tell your boyfriend or girlfriend you don't want to have sex yet, or you tell your friends you don't want to try the drugs they were planning on getting this weekend, you might experience difficulties in your relationships. But when you have good self-esteem, you know that you deserve the respect you're showing yourself by acting in accordance with your values, and you can feel good about yourself for doing this, even if it means you lose some friends or your partner breaks up with you. (When you don't yet have good self-esteem, you can get there by telling yourself these things.)

Acting in accordance with your core values is about being the person you want to be, rather than giving in to the pressure of trying to be the person others might want you to be. And as you do this, over time, you will start to feel better about yourself as a person.

Taking an Attitude of Gratitude

This is a skill that can help you act according to your core values. Consider what your life might be like if you didn't have what you have: your parents, your siblings, the place where you live, the friends you have, the school you go to, and so on. What would your life be like if you lived in a country ravaged by famine where you wouldn't have to worry about getting into college, because you might starve to death before you turn eighteen? What would your life be like if you lived in a war-torn nation, where you wouldn't have to worry about the fight you had with your friend yesterday, because when you woke up today you found his house had been blown up by a suicide bomber?

These examples might sound harsh. They are—but they are also reality for many people across the world. Thinking in this way can help put things back into perspective so that you can get a better handle on what really matters; and this can help you act in accordance with your values and be less judgmental. It can help you notice the things your parents are doing to support you, rather than focusing on the fact that they said no to your request to stay out after curfew this weekend. It can help you feel grateful for the one friend you do have in your life, rather than focusing on and judging yourself for the fact that you have only one friend. What are the things you're grateful for?

Building Mastery

Another skill that can help you increase your self-esteem is what we refer to as *building mastery*. This is about doing an activity that helps you feel a sense of pride or accomplishment; you feel good about yourself for what you've done. Because this skill is about the feeling rather than the activity, the activity or action that will lead to building mastery will vary from person to person. For Caitlyn, building mastery might mean going to all of her classes today; it might mean practicing a mindfulness exercise to help her manage her anxiety more effectively in the long run; or it could mean calling the new girl she met at school today and asking how her first day was. For Carter, building mastery might mean noticing when he's starting to get angry and leaving the room instead of blowing up; it could mean playing his guitar; or it might mean starting to exercise.

The idea with building mastery isn't the activity itself, but the feeling it brings you, so the activity could really be anything, as long as it gives you that feeling of accomplishment and pride in yourself for whatever it is that you've achieved. What might building mastery look like for you? Once you've identified an activity, don't stop there! Ideally, you want to be doing one thing *every single day* that gives you this feeling; over time, this will help you increase your self-esteem.

Increasing Friendships

Of course, the focus of this book being relationships, it's important to mention that increasing the number of (and improving) your friendships—and relationships in general—is also going to help you feel good about yourself and improve your self-esteem. This is a big topic, so let's start with what you've already got.

Deepening Current Relationships

First of all, it's important to realize that there are many different types of relationships and friendships. You might have acquaintances—people you know, but wouldn't consider friends and don't see them outside of their current context (for example, school or your martial arts club or the soccer league you play in).

Then you might have people you consider friends, but not close friends. These are the people you might call to go to the movies or the mall with you on the weekend, but they're not people who know that you have social anxiety, or that your parents are talking about separating, or any of the other really difficult things going on in your life because you don't feel comfortable sharing that much with them.

That brings us to your supports. Hopefully you have at least one person you can confide in and talk to, even if you don't do this all the time—that is, you know that person is there for you if you need him. I've purposely labeled this as "support" to be general, because this person could be a friend but it could also be a teacher, coach, or guidance counselor; it could be a parent or your sibling; it could be a religious leader, a therapist, or a close family friend—really, it could be anyone. So think for a moment about the supports you have in your life.

If you're a person who doesn't have many friends or support people, it's important to work on increasing this group. As humans, we are social creatures; we're not meant to be alone, and being socially isolated is unhealthy for us both emotionally and physically. So keeping this in mind, I hope that you will consider making a commitment to working on this as a goal for yourself.

If you're able to make this commitment, the first step is to consider how you might deepen any existing relationships. Consider your acquaintances—the people you play sports with, go to school with, work with, are on the debate team or in Spanish Club with—and think about whether there is someone with whom you might be able to form more of a connection. Maybe there's someone who had reached out to you once before, but because of your social anxiety you declined the invitation to the movies; or maybe there's someone you regularly sit beside at band practice, so it wouldn't seem that out of the ordinary if you tried to talk to him a bit more. This is typically the easiest place to start, so give it some thought and see if you can set a small goal for yourself. If you draw a blank here, of course, there are other options.

Rekindling Old Friendships

If you can't think of a way to deepen a connection with someone already in your life, here's your next thing to consider: is there anyone you used to be closer to and could consider reconnecting with? It's important to recognize that friendships wax and wane—sometimes you're close to a person, and then for whatever reason you drift apart. That doesn't mean the friendship is over; there wasn't necessarily a falling-out. It just means that your lives headed in different directions. And just because this happened doesn't mean you can't reconnect with that person and develop a friendship with him again. So think about it: is there anyone in your life who fits the bill?

If so, consider how you might go about reconnecting. Social media? E-mail? A phone call? Maybe he's still in your chemistry class and you can just go talk to him. Now's the time to practice mindfulness, of course: Don't think about how your reaching out might look to the other person. As best as you can, stay in the present, rather than worrying that your old friend will think it's weird that you're suddenly seeking him out. When you notice yourself trying to anticipate his reaction, bring yourself back to the here and now. This is about being more effective in your life, and better relationships through reconnection are a possibility, so you owe it to yourself to give reconnecting a chance.

Having said all that, of course, keep in mind that you can't control the outcome, and here's where your values come into play. Give it your best shot, treat yourself and your old friend respectfully, and work on being okay with the outcome, whatever it is. Worst-case scenario, he becomes angry with you, maybe says something hurtful and walks away; but best-case scenario, you might rekindle an old friendship and have someone playing a closer role in your life.

Looking for New Friendships

If you can't think of anyone you might want to deepen a relationship with or rekindle a friendship with, your last option—and often the most difficult—is to look for new friendships. I say this is often the most difficult because it involves going out of your comfort zone even further and meeting new people.

How might you do this? Sign up for a new activity at school that will get you interacting with people you don't know—join a drama club or an outdoors club; sign up to be on a fundraising committee. Or join an activity outside of school altogether—go skating at the community center; join a gym or sign up for classes at a dance school. Once you get into the activity, of course, you need to work hard on developing new relationships. Think about ways you can break the ice and start talking to others. Of the people you meet, consider who might have the potential to be a new friend, and when you do meet someone with potential, think about how you can purposely nurture this new connection.

You might be surprised at how far a simple smile can go. Smile at others and pay attention to the results: Do people smile back? Do they initiate conversations? Once you've smiled at someone and that person has smiled back, you might find that it tends to happen again the next time you see each other. Notice this. Pay attention to how you feel when you're smiling at others, and when they smile in return.

It's also important to remember that not everyone is going to like us, and we won't like everyone. This sometimes takes a lot of acceptance, and again goes back to core values—even if you don't like someone, work on treating him with respect. Remembering that everyone wants to be happy and is trying to be happy can help you understand others and their behavior.

Nurturing Your New Relationships

Once you've started to develop new friendships or to rekindle old ones, remember that they take work; you need to continue to nurture the relationships so they turn into healthy ones.

Setting Healthy Limits

In chapter 2 we looked briefly at how important it is to set healthy limits in order to have healthy, satisfying relationships with others. Setting healthy limits is about having a good balance of giving to and taking from others, rather than regularly doing one or the other, which burns the relationship out. In chapter 3 we talked in depth about how being able to communicate assertively will help you set and stick to healthier limits for yourself. You might want to go back and review both these sections to remind yourself of how important it is to set limits and communicate assertively in order to maintain healthy interactions.

If you can be healthy in your new friendships from the get-go, your life will be much easier and your interactions will go more smoothly, because these expectations are set out from the beginning. Think of it this way: we essentially train others (just as they train us) how to be in relationships with us. So if you meet someone and begin to develop a relationship with him, and come to feel that, like Rebecca, you need to bend over backward to do things for him in order to get him to want to become friends with you, you're teaching him that you will be the primary giver in the friendship, and that you'll often not want anything in return. Remember, the key for healthy relationships is balance—you want to give and take—so as best as you can, teach your new friend what that balance will look like. Sometimes you'll offer him a ride home from hockey practice, and sometimes you'll want him to drive. You'll buy coffee this week, and next week you'll remind him it's his turn. This is balanced; this is healthy.

Balancing Enjoyable Activities with Responsibilities

A final, important word here about working to maintain balance in your life and in your relationships: this is about balancing the things you do for yourself and the things you do because others demand them of you. Often we end up in conflict with others because the things we want to do for ourselves conflict with the things others want us to do; for example, Carter wants to practice with his new band, and Merrin wants him to spend an evening with her; Rebecca wants to sleep in, and her mother wants help with the grocery shopping.

Our world nowadays is a busy one and, as a teen, your life is probably super busy: between attending school and doing homework, trying to get some extracurricular activities in, doing volunteer work so your resume looks good for college, getting your chores done at home, maybe working a part-time job so you have some extra money, spending time with friends, reading this book your parents gave you to help you be more effective in your relationships... The list goes on and it can be really difficult to fit everything in. And although it's difficult, it's important to work to fit in both the things you want to do *and* the things you have to do. The good news is, the skills you've learned can really come in handy here, because they help you find a balance.

You can't be doing only the things you want to do, of course. Everyone has responsibilities, and in fact it's necessary for us to have responsibilities in order to feel needed and as though we have a purpose, and to be fulfilled in life. But of course, we also need to have things we do just for ourselves, because we want to do them—they're enjoyable, fun, relaxing, calming for us. If we didn't have these things, we'd be overwhelmed in life. Use your assertiveness skills to help you say no to demands that others are putting on you when you need to do something for yourself. But also use your wisdom to decide when you need to make a sacrifice for the health of your relationships. Remember balance: it can't always be about you, and it can't always be about the other person. And the more you work on finding this balance, the better you'll feel about yourself as you treat yourself and others with respect and dignity.

Your Next Steps

To continue with our theme of self-esteem in this chapter, here's a mindfulness exercise that helps you feel good about yourself and also helps you remind yourself of your values. This is called a loving-kindness meditation, and it helps you focus positive thoughts on yourself. (You can also direct it toward others.)

Exercise: Loving-Kindness Meditation

Find a place to sit where you'll be comfortable and able to focus. Start by bringing your attention to your breath—don't try to change it; just notice how it feels to breathe. Slowly, deeply, and comfortably, focus on your inhalations and exhalations. As you focus on your breath, allow yourself to connect with positive emotions—feelings of compassion, gentleness, kindness, and friendliness. These are the emotions that might come up when you see a person you really care about, when your pet climbs into your lap, or when you do something nice for someone for no particular reason.

Focus on the warmth and kindness you experience toward others; imagine those feelings right now, as though they were happening in this moment, and let yourself feel the joy, love, and other pleasurable feelings that come up for you. As you experience these feelings of kindness and caring, gently say the following words to yourself, directing them toward yourself:

May I be happy.

May I be healthy.

May I be peaceful.

May I be safe.

You can think these words to yourself in your head, or you can say them out loud; either way, make sure that, as best as you can, you really feel the words as you say them and you put feeling and meaning into each one. If it's difficult for you to feel kindness toward yourself, remember that habits take time to change, and as best as you can, don't judge yourself or the exercise; just know that this is something you'll need to spend more time on.

187

Make sure that you practice this exercise regularly, and you'll find that you're able to take a kinder, more loving, and gentler attitude toward yourself. Over time, this will help you to be less judgmental toward yourself, to validate the emotions you're feeling, to accept your reality—whatever it is—and to increase your self-esteem.

Conclusion

Relationships—with parents, friends, teachers, bosses, coaches, boyfriends or girlfriends, peers, or anyone else in your life—can be really difficult and complicated, and a huge source of emotional pain. But the reality is that, as humans, we need these relationships. We need to interact with others on a daily basis; we need social support; we need intimacy. And the happier and healthier our relationships are, the happier and healthier we will be.

In this book, you've read about a lot of skills that can help you interact with others and connect with others more effectively, and that can help you move your relationships in a healthier direction. Hopefully you're practicing these skills and becoming more aware of your strengths and difficulties so that you know what you need to do to move in a more balanced direction. But before we finish, there's still one last thing I want to teach you, which is directly related to where you go from here.

Willingness—Opening Yourself to Possibilities

You may have heard the saying "You need to play the cards you're dealt." Well, we're all dealt a certain hand in life. Some people develop mood or anxiety disorders; others are born with severe illnesses like cerebral palsy, autism, or muscular dystrophy. Some people end up having to deal with serious illnesses later in life, such as cancer, multiple sclerosis, or other debilitating diseases. Others don't have specific medical conditions to cope with, but have experienced traumas like car accidents, being victims of a crime or a natural disaster, and so on. The point is, you can't control what life throws at you; you have to play the cards you're dealt. If you don't, you end up making your own suffering worse by fighting reality—this is *willfulness*.

Willfulness is when you shut yourself off from possibilities, when you refuse to make any attempt to make things better for yourself. When you're willful, you essentially shut down, give up, throw in the towel; you toss up your hands and think, *Whatever, there's nothing I can do about it anyway*. When you're willful, you're closing yourself off from life; you're giving up hope.

Willingness is the opposite of willfulness: it's playing the cards you're dealt—even when those cards are really awful. You do the best you can with what you've got, even if you don't have much hope of winning the hand. Willingness is opening yourself up to possibilities, making the attempt to make things better even when things are really hard; it's holding on to hope and acting as skillfully as you can.

If you've done the work I've asked you to do in this book, you've been working on developing your self-awareness, and you may have seen some things in yourself that you're not too thrilled about. (Welcome to the human race!) Willingness is about working on accepting these things, and doing the best you can with the challenges you're facing in order to make your life a life worth living—whatever that might look like for you. But for all of us, a life worth living has to include connecting with others on some level, and I'm hoping that this is what you'll take from this concluding chapter: that even though things might be really difficult for you, and even if you've realized that you have some big changes you need to make in your life, or some obstacles that you might not be able to overcome, you'll keep trying anyway. Because one guarantee I can pretty much give you is that, in life, if you do give up, things aren't likely to get better.

Reassessing Your Interpersonal Effectiveness

I'd like you to take some time now to again complete the Interpersonal Effectiveness Self-Assessment that you completed at the beginning of this book. It will be helpful to take another look at where you're at now, not only to see whether you've made any changes since you've started using the skills you've learned but also to see if anything new has come into your awareness since you completed it the first time.

The Interpersonal Effectiveness Self-Assessment

Read each statement carefully, and put a check mark beside each one you think describes you. You may find that a statement applies to you *sometimes*; ask yourself if it applies to you *more often than not*, and if it does, put a check mark beside it.

Satisfaction with Relationships

_____ I feel like I don't have enough people in my life (friends, supportive family members, acquaintances, mentors, and so on).

_____ I don't have anyone I can talk with about it when I have a problem I don't know how to fix.

_____ I don't have anyone I can ask to hang out with me when I have no plans on a Saturday night.

Communication

_____ People in my life tell me that I don't communicate well.

_____ People I am close to complain that I don't open up to them.

_____ I tend to end relationships because they aren't going well without trying to fix the problems first.

Unhealthy Limits

_____ I feel like I either give or take more in my relationships, rather than having a balance of give *and* take.

_____ I feel taken advantage of in my relationships.

_____ I tend to get into unhealthy relationships (for example, having relationships with people who use drugs or drink a lot, or get into a lot of trouble with their parents or even the police; or having relationships with people who don't treat me well, bully me, and so on).

What did you find? Has anything changed for you in a positive direction? Or perhaps you've realized some things that you didn't realize the first time you completed this assessment. Maybe neither. Whatever the case, the good thing is you just practiced willingness in completing this questionnaire again in order to do everything you can to improve things for yourself.

Your Next Steps

First of all, congratulations on sticking to your commitment and making it to the last pages of this book! I hope that you've found this book helpful and that, even if you're not practicing all of the skills yet, they're at least starting to make sense to you and you've come to see some of the areas you need to work on. Remember, if you really want them to help, the skills you've learned aren't just ones you're going to practice a few times and then leave behind. They're lasting changes you need to make in your life, and so it makes sense that you'll need to read this book more than once. If you haven't taken notes or highlighted what you think are the important points, as suggested in the introduction, you can do that on a second reading. This is something you'll have to think about for yourself: how can you take the skills you've learned in these pages and insert them into your life in an effective way?

Remember to practice accessing your own wisdom and also to ask for help from the people you already have in your life. You're not alone in the problems you're experiencing, and when your loved ones see you working hard to make changes, I hope that they'll not only applaud you but also want to help in any way they can to see you become a healthier, happier person. And that's what these skills are about: helping you become happier and healthier, and moving you in the direction of a life worth living. It might sound clichéd, but believe me, I wish I had known when I was a teenager what I know now. They really should offer this course in school: Relationship Skills 101!

Sheri Van Dijk, MSW, is a psychotherapist in private practice and at Southlake Regional Health Centre in Newmarket, ON, Canada. She is author of *The Dialectical Behavior Therapy Skills Workbook for Bipolar Disorder, Don't Let Your Emotions Run Your Life for Teens, Calming the Emotional Storm,* and *DBT Made Simple,* and coauthor of *The Bipolar Workbook for Teens.* In September 2010, she received the R.O. Jones Award from the Canadian Psychiatric Association for her research on using dialectical behavior therapy (DBT) skills to treat bipolar disorder. Sheri presents internationally on using DBT to treat mental health problems.